This book is for Jim Campbell,
who always said I would get there in the end.

FISHERS OF MEN

FISHERS OF MEN

Rob Lewis

Hodder & Stoughton

First published in Great Britain in 1999
by Hodder and Stoughton

A division of Hodder Headline PLC

10 9 8 7 6 5 4 3 2 1

British Library Cataloguing in Publication Data
A CIP catalogue record for this title
is available from the British Library.

ISBN 0 340 75071 5

Typeset by Hewer Text Ltd, Edinburgh
Printed and bound in Great Britain by
Clays Ltd, St Ives plc

Hodder and Stoughton
A division of Hodder Headline PLC
338 Euston Road
London NW1 3BH

Author's Note

Owing to the sensitive nature of the contents of this book, a copy of the original manuscript was submitted to the Ministry of Defence prior to publication.

At their request, some changes were made to the text, including the alteration of the identities of individuals and locations, in order to protect the work of those who play a key role in the fight against terrorism.

Acknowledgments

The author would like to thank Mike Curtis for planting the seed for this project, Mike R. for his help at the start, and Ali for her enthusiasm and encouragement.

I would also mention the thanks I owe to my wife for her tolerance of my late-night writing sessions.

Contents

List of Illustrations

1. Sennelager, Germany. Northern Ireland riot training.
2. Sennelager, Germany.
3. Part of a weapons cache found in Omagh, Northern Ireland.
4. Munitions from the weapons cache found in Omagh, Northern Ireland.
5. Children playing in a field in Strabane, Northern Ireland.
6. Strabane, Northern Ireland.
7. Inside base, Strabane, Northern Ireland.
8. Hunger strikers at the Maze prison, Omagh, Northern Ireland. (PA News)
9. A now defunct airport, Nicosia, Cyprus.
10. The infamous 'Free Derry' wall, Londonderry, Northern Ireland.
11. Close Quarter Battle training, Ashford, Kent.
12. Vehicle drills on the FRU course, Ashford, Kent.
13. CQB training, Ashford, Kent.
14. CQB training, Ashford, Kent.
15. The Remembrance Day bomb, Enniskillen, Northern Ireland. (PA News)

Foreword

When the Troubles in Northern Ireland began thirty years ago various military units were hastily formed to undertake the unenviable task of carrying out reactive intelligence operations against the terrorist groupings within the Province. Over a period of some years the organisation of these agencies had been completed, so that by the early 1980s a definitive intelligence-gathering system was in force. The task of agent-handling was delegated to the newly formed Force Research Unit (FRU) under the command of the Director of Intelligence. The objective of the unit was to target, recruit and run human sources from all divisions of the community, with priority given to the running of agents within the terrorist organisations themselves.

The FRU's role is probably the most sensitive of all the covert operations undertaken within Northern Ireland. It is the only military unit that exploits pre-emptive intelligence gathered directly from its informants to combat terrorist activity.

The unit's operators are volunteers from all three services and the arduous selection process is open to both male and female applicants. Unlike other agencies that carry out similar roles within the Province the FRU does not advertise its requirement for candidates on service orders, the existence of the unit is hardly known throughout the armed forces, and media coverage of its activities has remained very scant and invariably inaccurate.

The unit is commanded by a lieutenant-colonel and is subdivided into detachments covering specific geographical areas of responsibility. Each detachment is commanded by a captain. The operators are all senior non-commissioned officers.

Operators from the FRU have been awarded more gallantry awards and commendations than any other unit in Northern Ireland.

Prologue

At seven o'clock precisely my team were all deployed in their positions. All had reported their locations to the operations room and were awaiting the radio message from the operator who would hopefully have the first physical contact with Declan. We expected to hear a quick, straightforward transmission to the effect that the subject was through his area and heading to where we were positioned.

Every member of the team carried their own personal weapon, a Browning 9mm automatic pistol. In addition to this basic requirement all of us carried a Heckler and Koch 5.56mm machinegun with folding stock, spare magazines, smoke grenades and first-aid packs. The possible dangers of a new-source recruitment are unknown, and this operation was being carried out only a short distance from an area where we knew that the Provisionals had carried out attacks on previous occasions. All the firearms and equipment that the team carried were hidden well out of sight but could easily be brought into action in a split second, if required.

Fifteen minutes had passed and there was no sign of Declan. No calls had been made to the phone number I had given him,

Rob Lewis

and so I pushed the radio pressel switch. 'All call signs, this is Romeo. Go mobile, return to your start locations at twenty hundred hours. All call signs confirm. Over.' All the team came up individually and confirmed that they had received the message and were driving out of the area.

Half an hour had passed and so, with as much speed as we could muster, we headed back to the locations we had been in previously. The team chattered away on the radio, informing each other of their chosen routes back into the area.

The boss's voice came up on the radio from our operations room. He informed us that a report had come in from a Close Observation Team (COT) to the west of our position, stating that they believed they had observed unidentified armed men moving around approximately one kilometre to their east. That would make their position very close to us. I toyed with the idea of aborting the operation, but decided against it. They were unable to give any more information but would try to keep us fully informed of any new developments. My adrenalin level shot through the roof, and just for my own peace of mind I checked that each of my weapons, the Browning pistol and the Heckler and Koch, was 'ready'. I gently released the safety catch and pulled back the cocking slide on the pistol and saw the glint of brass in the chamber. I knew it was loaded, but I had to check anyway. Everyone else on the job probably did exactly the same. Declan was really an unknown quantity. I sat in my vehicle and thought of the consequences of a set-up. I made sure that the interior light was switched off and gently eased the door open. If I had to get away quickly that would be one obstacle less to deal with.

I slowly brought the Heckler and Koch up from my side and laid it across my lap. I had trained with it hundreds of times, but as I sat there I thumbed the safety catch on and off in anticipation of the worst. My eyes were all over the place –

looking in front, checking the rear-view mirror, glancing to both sides in an awkward way, straining to catch sight of any movement around me in the dusk. I quietly whistled to myself, something I had always done when I knew things were not quite right. It was my way of letting myself know I was nervous.

Chapter 1

'Train up a child in the way he
should go, and when he is old,
he will not depart from it'

Proverbs 22:6

My home town was a rather grey mining village located in the middle valleys area of South Wales, situated midway between the heavy industrial area of Merthyr Tydfil in the north and the historic town of Caerphilly in the south. It had a resemblance to the town in *How Green Was My Valley*, but with a few stark differences to that romantic portrayal of life in the valleys. The coal-blackened faces of the miners winding their way home from their shifts underground were certainly there. However, there was no sign of them singing their hearts out as they were greeted by their loving wives at the front doors of their houses, nor were there smiling children ready with a tin bath full of hot soapy water in front of a roaring fire to wash their fathers' backs. In this town the miners were more likely to have gone straight into the local pub and to have been physically dragged out by their spouses later in the day, the women determined to get their housekeeping money safely in their purses as opposed to filling the coffers of the local public-house landlords. These were hard men in many ways, with wives to equal them.

When I was a youngster growing up in the South Wales valleys it seemed like the best place on earth. We had our well-trusted gang of friends, we had a vast expanse of mountain area to explore, and we had the run of the busy town. We also had a number of other places, like the local mine-workers' institute and the colliery, in which to amuse ourselves. This was our patch, and we jealously guarded it against all outsiders. Fights between gangs of youths from rival villages and towns were commonplace and were often quite violent. During these pitched battles it was not unusual for serious injuries to be inflicted. One teenage lad from a village north of our town had a near escape when he was thrown from the bridge over the railway line. The police arrived and dragged him off the line just a few moments before the Merthyr to Cardiff train would have sliced straight through him. The town had built up a notoriety that was soon to be brought to the attention of the gangs in the larger places like Cardiff and Caerphilly. A showdown was destined to happen. Late on a particular Friday night the packed-out Cardiff train pulled into the local station and spilled out its load of invaders. They were greeted with a hail of bottles, bricks, iron bars and whatever else was throwable. The large crowd that had come to give the youth of our town a lesson were soon on their way home.

From the very start of my teenage years life was just good fun, marred only by the unfortunate requirement to attend school. The school had been founded at the beginning of the century and had started its career in the higher elementary role. It was regarded as a fine specimen of selective education for post-primary pupils. It had been formally recognised as a secondary school some years later, and had become a grammar school in the years just after the First World War. To me it was a large, daunting, redbrick building where the only objective of the black-gowned teachers was to see how many times a day they could have me stood outside the headmaster's office for an inevitable caning. From day one it seemed that every teacher knew me intimately, the unfortunate legacy of having an elder brother at the same school, a brother who had gained a reputation that was too easily passed on. I was destined to be the target of certain teachers' attentions, but not always to the benefit of my education. In my fourth and fifth years at grammar school I would regularly wear two pairs of underpants, my swimming trunks and a pair of rugby shorts under my grey school trousers in an effort to minimise the stinging pain of the bamboo stick. This was all very well until the headmaster who dealt out the punishment, a red-faced authoritarian, changed his tactics and administered the cane across the palm of the hand. I would bend over in readiness. This worked sometimes, but on other occasions the sight of my well-padded buttocks probably influenced his decision to dispense the penalty across my fingers instead.

Our little gang would get up to all kinds of mischief and misdemeanours, which were probably to stand me in good stead for the future. My home town and the surrounding area was an excellent training ground for a potential life of running, hiding, sneaking about and being able to talk oneself out of a dilemma. Our pack of friends consisted of about ten lads. To any adults, teachers and outsiders who knew us then, what our band of scoundrels managed to achieve in later life would probably convince even the greatest sceptic that anything is possible for subjects of a misspent youth. Our merry bunch of no-hopers managed to turn out two special forces soldiers, an executive with Plessey in New York, a teacher in Canada, an Olympic athlete, a recipient of the MBE, a first-class rugby player, a commissioned officer in the army, a company director in London, a police inspector, and another who has a 'shady' job in Whitehall. Not bad going for a bunch of lads from working-class backgrounds in a high-unemployment area of the South Wales coalmining valleys. There were many others from the same background living in the same town who ended up in correction centres and prisons for their various misdemeanours. It could easily have gone that way for any of us. Being a somewhat outgoing and boisterous bunch, we were more often than not involved in some kind of nonsense which could quite easily have led us into trouble on many occasions. More often than not, though, we were able to get away scot-free.

Most weekends we would engage in the usual local teenage prank of setting the numerous gorse bushes up on the mountain on fire. After the initial thick grey smoke had run its course the fire would then take full hold and burn ferociously. It could easily be seen for many miles – when you have about ten bushes burning simultaneously it is quite a sight, an absolute Mecca for trainee arsonists. We would head for the nearest telephone, ring the fire brigade in the town and test their reaction times in getting to the area and putting the fires out. We would even go and talk to the firemen and give them detailed descriptions of non-existent youths whom we had seen running away from the scene of the crime. Maybe I would be naïve to think that they believed a word we said. However, even when the police arrived to see what was happening, we always kept to the same story, although we always made a point of dumping the matches along the route first in case they decided to tell us to turn our pockets out.

One of our little gang's regular Saturday afternoon activities was 'nicking'. The general idea was to split into groups of two lads, make our way into the town and steal the most useless or the largest item we could get away with within the timescale laid down, then return to the park shed to compare our booty. Howls of laughter came from the shed when the various trophies were presented. I still smile at the memory of seeing everything from pineapples, sets of cutlery, bicycle pumps and even a pitchfork laid out in front of us while we compared notes on how we had nearly got caught, discussed how a particular shop-owner was getting wise to us entering his shop every Saturday, and what the plan would be for the following weekend's nicking trip.

This hobby was to progress to the stage where many years later two members of our gang, at a friend's stag party, relieved the local transport company of a fifty-six-seater luxury coach. After demolishing a bus stop *en route*, the said article was last seen in the middle of an Essex county cricket ground with its four-way flashing hazard lights on, and in the distance yells of 'Fares, please' from the two culprits could be heard as they fled into the darkness, pursued unsuccessfully by the local constabulary. As can be imagined, that night's activity has often given us a great laugh since. It also reinforced a point that had been our gang's adopted motto for many years. Rule one: don't get caught.

Unfortunately getting caught did happen on one or two occasions. One time I remember being caught out well and truly was at the local mine-workers' institute. This was another typical South Wales valleys redbrick building, where the miners had a snooker hall upstairs and various function rooms downstairs, including a ballroom that doubled up as a bingo hall for a few evenings a week. Two or three of us had been playing snooker upstairs when it was noticed that the man who ran the place, Old Maxwell, was nowhere to be seen. As quick as a flash my two companions moved to the far end of the hall where the doorway to the caretaker's accommodation was located, while I grabbed a chair and very quickly started to empty the glass case over the counter of all the Aeros and Mars bars I could lay my hands on. I looked over at one of my mates, who gave me the thumbs-up. It was still all clear. Just as I was about to move to the area that contained the cigarette packets I heard a shout of 'What the hell are you up to?'

Fucking hell! Old Maxwell had come into the hall through the back door. My comrades had not seen him coming. He came directly over to where I was stood on the chair and swiftly grabbed my leg. I did my best impression of a forward roll off the chair, slapped the floor with my hand, and began to yell out in feigned agony. The initial grim and annoyed look on his face turned to one of sheer panic. I rolled about, yelling loudly and pretending to have an asthma attack. Old Maxwell became extremely concerned, and it was a real effort for me to carry on the charade. I tried hard not to laugh out loud. One of my friends walked in and made it quite clear to Old Maxwell that he was really in the shit for grabbing my leg and accused him of hitting me, which of course he hadn't. My mate told him that it was likely that, when my father was told of this, he would probably come and give him a good hiding for attacking me. The man was apologetic in the extreme. I sobbed, limped and gasped for breath as I asked him for a drink, and suggested that if I could move to the door for some fresh air it would probably help my breathing recover. He agreed this was probably a good idea and told me to go outside, adding that he would fetch me a drink of water. As my two comrades assisted me to the door one whispered to me, asking if I was OK. I said of course I was, I was putting it on; at this point the three of us turned and shouted at Old Maxwell, telling him what a gullible old git he had been, and ran off down the street. No Equity cards required here. We were all natural actors. It was quite some time before I returned to play snooker, though.

Another great expedition that we embarked on from time to time was to venture down to the area of the local colliery. My grandfather had worked at this colliery in its heyday. It was situated in the valley of the local river to the east of the town, and the works area stretched over several miles, consisting largely of heavy machinery houses, pithead baths, mine shafts, dynamite stores and blacksmiths' shops. To a bunch of young teenage lads like us it really was an Aladdin's cave, although in reality it was an extremely dangerous place to be.

The colliery in those days was the working environment for about three thousand men, operating over a number of different shifts twenty-four hours a day. These men became known to our gang as 'the enemy'. One of our favourite jaunts was to catch the empty coal drams at the top end of the colliery, jump aboard, ride on them until they were approaching the pithead area of the works and then jump off at the last minute to avoid being caught by the enemy. This was actually a necessity, as the miners really would give you a damned good thumping if they caught you. They knew the risks and dangers of our little joyrides; we did not. These drams were extremely heavy four-wheeled steel containers for carrying loads of coal along a rail track. One false move or fall and they could quite easily have cut straight through a limb like a hot knife through butter. After one particularly fun-filled afternoon of coal-dram riding I decided to head home. On the way it became evident that my shoes were caked black with coal dust, and I thought that if my parents were to cotton on to the fact that I had been down in the area of the colliery then the smelly stuff really would hit the fan. Along with the rest of the intrepid gang I made my way to the pithead baths, where, just inside the doors, were positioned two industrial boot cleaners for the miners to grease and polish their heavy steel-toed pit boots. After a quick spin under the revolving brushes my shoes would have passed the scrutiny of any Guardsman, and I made my way home thinking that I was looking spick and span. I was very wrong.

As I walked down the garden path and into the house my mother took one look at me, shouted at me to get out and then proceeded to give me a mild bollocking about going down to play in the area of the colliery. I remember looking at her in complete amazement and stating quite categorically that I had been nowhere near the place – if I had been down the colliery, then how come my shoes were so clean? She then told me to go to the bathroom and take a look in the mirror. The sight in front of me was reminiscent of old films and photographs I had seen of the young lads who worked underground, or of chimney-sweep kids. I was filthy with coal dust. Lesson learnt – if you are going to lie, make sure you have your alibi watertight. Attention to detail is a necessity. On future occasions when we had been down the colliery we used to go home via the open-air swimming pool in the town and use their showers. My mother never caught me out again.

It was a cold, damp Sunday afternoon, and I was about thirteen at the time. After making sure that all signs of coal dust had been eradicated from my face I sat down to watch the television while my mother started to prepare tea. The evening news commenced with the story of another riot in Northern Ireland. I had never really paid that much attention to the problems in a province I knew very little about, and cared nothing about for that matter. I vaguely remember my parents saying how terrible it all was – that was about it for me. This particular Sunday was different, though. It was 1972 and this was the last Sunday in January, Bloody Sunday. The thought of ever being involved personally in any shape or form with the Province never entered my mind. Why should it? Although I knew that thirteen people had been shot by the army that day, the realities of the situation went straight over my head. I do remember seeing film coverage of teenagers of my age throwing stones and the occasional petrol bomb at the army. I wondered if they had bollockings off their mothers as well. I suppose I was lucky to live and grow up where I did. I felt a certain sympathy for those kids – life must have been bloody awful in those conditions. The following day we played soldiers and rioters in the schoolyard. Ironically, I was a rioter.

I was lucky enough to have had numerous family holidays in the seaside town of Porthcawl, a traditional 'miner's fortnight' in the last week of July and the first week of August. My grandparents owned a caravan there, and more often than not I would stay on for a few extra weeks with them.

My scallywag ways were to turn into profitable ventures working at the funfairs at Trecco Bay and Coney Beach, both packed-out places of entertainment during these periods. Along with the other lads working at the fair I would remove all the seats from the various rides in the mornings and coat the base with a thick green slime of Swarfega, a substance usually used for cleaning dirty or oily hands. It was also an excellent way to catch coins that had fallen from the pockets of the people who had been on the various rides. At closedown every evening a few minutes was spent washing off the slimy coins, which were then added to my pay and holiday money. A lucrative little number indeed.

Porthcawl, as well as being a great place for families wanting a decent holiday, was also sometimes a magnet for people looking for trouble. With some concern for my own safety I watched one afternoon as a large group of Hell's Angels went haywire along the arcades and public houses in Coney Beach, turning tables over, smashing fruit machines open and grabbing young girls as they tried to escape. There were about forty of them in total, rampaging their way along to one of the large pubs along the seafront. They looked extremely menacing. Most were long-haired, dirty, tattooed and drunk, a few wore World War II German helmets, and all had cut-off denim jackets over their leathers proclaiming 'Windsor' in Gothic writing. This was a chapter that over the years has gained quite a notorious reputation. Two policemen who approached them were forced to back off as a variety of chains and knives were openly displayed, and it was more than obvious that the Angels would have been quite happy to use them. Then the group descended on a large pub with a huge outside seating area for families. This was their biggest mistake. As dangerous and as wild as they were, they had not bargained on a major factor of Porthcawl at this time of the year – the Welsh miner.

I had followed them down along the tarmac path leading from the funfair towards the caravan park. They then proceeded to turn and force their way through families having a quiet afternoon drink in the sun. The whole area erupted. Women and kids were forced over to a grassed patch while about fifty or sixty 'sports jackets' suddenly stood up and went to town on the gang. It was mayhem. I watched as a large broad-shouldered man stamped on the face of one of the gang who had been punched to the floor by another bloke sat at the same table. The most amusing part was that, as he was stamping on him, he was talking to him. He was actually telling him that he had spoilt his day and really should not have done what he had done. This was not uncontrolled rage – the bloke was explaining to the Hell's Angel quite calmly where he had gone wrong. The fact that his face was splattered all over the place and he appeared to be unconscious did not matter. After about ten minutes the whole thing calmed down, and the police finally had enough back-up to bring some control to the scene. The Windsor chapter sauntered away, bloodied and beaten, and the sports jackets sat down and carried on drinking as if nothing had happened. Another lesson to be learnt — no matter how hard you may think you are, you do not fuck with a bunch of Welsh miners when they are on holiday with their families. These were hard men, really hard, and this was the environment I was brought up in.

The holidays came to an end and my school examinations loomed, and with them the usual unanswerable question of what my possible future employment would be. The subject was constantly being raised by teachers and my parents. I was having too much fun with my friends to be interested in studying and was subsequently no bright light in school. Therefore the choices open to me were really going to be limited. An apprenticeship with the National Coal Board was an option, but it did not really appeal to me. I had no idea which way I was likely to go until one weekend when my elder brother returned on leave from the army with three of his mates. That weekend was to have a profound effect on me and confirmed what I wanted for my future.

My brother had been the first soldier in our family for several generations. During World War II both my grandfathers had had commitments in the coalmines under what was termed reserved employment, whereby even if they had wanted to join up their jobs as mine-workers restricted them to the colliery. My maternal great-grandfather was the only soldier I was aware of in a direct blood-line. He had won the Distinguished Conduct Medal at the Somme while serving with the 2nd Battalion, The Welsh Regiment. He was in his late thirties at the time, and probably went to war because the money was better than in mining. He paid the price for his actions, though, and spent a long period of time on his return recuperating after being mustard-gassed by the Germans during the trench warfare that was the horrendous trademark of that campaign.

I was completely overwhelmed by the friendship and loyalty my brother and his mates showed towards each other. They would do each other's ironing, lend each other clothes and money, and they all looked very fit and suntanned, having just returned from an exercise in Canada. And if pushed into a corner they were more than capable of looking after themselves, either as individuals or as a group. I had a good bunch of school-mates who were great fun, and we stuck together, but these four were way beyond the level of friendship I had with them. Before the week was out I had spoken to my father and told him of my intentions. It was not a problem for him or my mother – I think they were quietly happy about my decision after seeing what my brother had achieved – but because I was underage for adult service, I needed his permission and his signature on the forms to allow me to join up. I think he was quite pleased that after so many years of being a bit of a daydreamer and obviously not being destined to go to Oxbridge I had made a decision for myself. Even if it was influenced by circumstances close to home, this was the first positive sign I had shown for some time. I had initially wanted to join my brother's regiment straight away, but the four of them convinced me that I should join a corps first and gain a trade. If I still wanted to go into their regiment after that, then at least I would have something to fall back on for the future should things not turn out for the best. It made sense.

My father and I travelled to the army careers office in Cardiff, and I went through the various tests and interviews to gain entry as a junior soldier. Surprisingly, I passed all the tests with flying colours and was given the option of entering any arm or service, with a range of trades on offer, from taking up employment in the Army Air Corps as a helicopter mechanic through to being a Pioneer Corps trench-digger. I opted for a middle-of-the-road choice and took my oath of allegiance to Queen and country.

That September I arrived at the army Apprentice College in Chepstow, not a million miles from home but far enough away for a new start in adult life. I was to embark on a two-year apprenticeship as a plant operator and mechanic with the Royal Engineers. Chepstow offered a good learning curve for a sometimes wayward sixteen-year-old, but there was still something missing. The soldiers in the corps I was with did not have the same bond of comradeship I had seen in my brother and his mates. There was just something that I could never quite put my finger on which made them different. After a while I began to get itchy feet.

I decided that after finishing my apprenticeship I would transfer to my brother's regiment and join the Royal Armoured Corps. During the period after finishing at Chepstow I was at the School of Engineering in Chatham, Kent, completing my City and Guilds in plant engineering, when I approached the adjutant and told him about my wish to transfer. He completely dismissed my request and told me that because of the amount of money invested in my training by the corps I was destined to stay with the Royal Engineers for a minimum period of three years. Wrong. The British Army has some strange and ancient traditions, one of which is an historic rule that allows brothers, sons and fathers to 'claim' their blood relatives into whichever regiment or corps they are in — with the consent of both parties, of course. So, with the shake of a short stick, I was on my way to Catterick Garrison in Yorkshire, much to the annoyance of my sapper adjutant.

Catterick at the time was the Royal Armoured Corps training centre. It was where newly joined up recruits went through what the army calls Basic Military Training. This includes a period of drill, weapons handling followed by drill, bed-pack-making with a hint of drill, and when there were periods between bulling boots and being shouted at there would always be the opportunity for a short period of more drill.

After this initial 'beasting' period the recruits then progressed to trade training. My contemporaries at Chepstow had moved on to their basic military training at the Royal Engineers Training Regiment in Dover, Kent, while I had been at Chatham. I would have been due to follow them into this abyss after completing my exams. It was time for me to put to the test my well-honed skills at bluff and double bluff. With all the brass neck I could muster, I strolled in to the chief clerk's office of the resident armoured corps training regiment and announced myself as Sapper Lewis, recently transferred from the Royal Engineers at Chatham for trade training with his regiment, prior to posting. He immediately took my bundle of paperwork and documents and rang the guardroom and informed them that I was to be allocated a single room in the permanent staff block away from the recruits. The grin on my face on the walk up to the block would have put the proverbial Cheshire cat to shame. I had managed to sneak through the net and into the regular army without having to go through the drill and bullshit of basic training. I wonder how many other soldiers can claim the same?

Trade training progressed, and after passing the various phases in the driving and basic maintenance of tracked vehicles I moved on to the signals wing to complete my basic radio course. I collected my posting order to Germany soon after. By the middle of August 1978 I was in Hohne Garrison, near Bergen-Belsen, in a reconnaissance regiment equipped with Scimitar and Scorpion light armoured vehicles. Hohne was not exactly the best place in the world. It was home to a few thousand troops from a variety of countries, including Americans and Dutch conscripts. The latter were the butt of endless ribbing from the British troops. They were quite well equipped, had casually styled uniforms, and most resembled Anneka Rice with their long, flowing blond hair. They invariably sauntered around the garrison with cigarettes dangling from the sides of their mouths and were not the slightest bit interested in being soldiers. I often toyed with the idea of doing a runner to Amsterdam, claiming asylum, and returning to Hohne as a 'Cloggie' conscript soldier, so I could walk around camp with my hands in my pockets and a strange-smelling roll-up cigarette dangling precariously from my lips.

Hohne was also home to several other British Army regiments. It also contained the sum total of one nightclub, which was frequented by all parties. Friday and Saturday nights were always the scene of pitched battles between rival units, a bit like being back home, really. The club concerned made a fortune in overpriced beer sales, which probably more than adequately covered the cost of the glasses smashed every night and the windows that were caved in by flying bar stools from time to time. It really was the stuff of television western-style bar-room brawls. However, this was for real. It was not unusual to go out into the early morning light after leaving the club to see a line of blue flashing lights on vehicles belonging to Military Police representatives from several NATO countries who were helping the German civilian police to keep the soldiers from their various nations in order, a job they were most welcome to.

For the first few years my view of the army was distorted by the fact that all the places I had been so far were training establishments. Lance-corporals ran around shouting, corporals walked about shouting, sergeants stood still and pointed while they shouted, and everyone was scared shitless of the guy who was known as the sergeant-major. Officers never spoke to you properly. The only contact I really made with any officers was when I saluted them as I moved around camp and said 'Good morning' or 'Good afternoon, sir', which was invariably ignored other than for a pathetic reciprocal salute. After three years I still did not actually know what officers did. Twenty-three years later I could probably still toss a coin over that one.

With this distorted view it was an amazing shock to the system to arrive at my new regiment on a Friday afternoon to find the squadron I was joining in the throes of a 'happy hour'. This time-honoured tradition consisted of everyone leaving the cookhouse on a Friday lunch-time and going straight into the squadron bar. All ranks from troopers through to warrant officer, from second lieutenant to major, were in the bar, all in work dress, and all drinking and having a laugh together.

I was greeted at the squadron block by my brother and two of his mates, whom I knew well from their previous stays at my parents' home. My cases were unceremoniously dumped in the clerk's office and I was taken to the squadron bar. There were handshakes all round and a load of introductions made; things were looking very good. One of the first introductions was to my new squadron sergeant-major, the man with the dreaded rank. He looked at me, asked me what I wanted to drink and then proceeded to give me my welcome interview to the squadron there and then, in the bar. This chat was swiftly followed by my introduction to the squadron leader, a major by rank, who tapped me on the shoulder and asked me if I was as handy a rugby player as my brother was. This appeared to be his main concern. He told me that he hoped I would be turning out regularly for both the squadron and regimental teams. The icing on the cake, after he had brought me my drink, was to ask me which troop I fancied going to. What the hell was going on here?

The choice of troop he gave me was quite laughable. In his well-toned but slightly drink-slurred upper-class voice, he informed me that 2nd Troop were off to Berlin, 'for a jolly', 3rd Troop were off to the South of France canoeing for two weeks, and I could make my own choice as to which troop I wished to join. The following week saw me in the French sunshine with 3rd Troop for two weeks. The canoes appeared once for the obligatory photograph for the regimental journal and were never seen again until we returned to Hohne.

Exercises came and went. I enjoyed being out of camp with my new troop on these various military schemes and found myself starting to want to progress within my squadron. I had managed to convince my troop leader to give me the chance of moving out of the driver's seat into the turret and becoming a radio operator. I quickly learnt that if you wanted to get noticed and promoted you had to be seen and heard. Staying cooped up in the driver's seat of an armoured vehicle is not the best place to be for this. Range periods came and went as well, and I found that gunnery was enjoyable as well as being a necessary requirement for gaining promotion. I was determined to get on the first rung of the ladder. I was promoted to lance-corporal, and soon after, in my usual style, I was reduced in rank back to trooper. Our troop had been laid up for the night and we had worked out the rota for radio watch during the small hours. I was due to be on duty from four in the morning until five, and so got my head down for the night. The bloke I would be taking over from would give me a shout just prior to me taking over the radio watch. The wake-up call did not come; the bloke concerned had fallen asleep during his stag. We had a visit from one of the exercise-directing staff at half past four and yours truly was fast asleep inside a lovely warm sleeping bag. On return to camp I was marched in front of the commanding officer, bollocked, fined, reduced in rank and marched out. Easy as that. No explanation was offered by me as it was bound to fall on stony ground. The fat bastard who failed to stay awake for his duty said nothing.

True to form, and with a macabre sense of humour found only in the forces, I was greeted by a mate of mine walking down the corridor after I had just been marched out by the regimental sergeant-major (RSM). As we approached each other he burst into song. The song was 'Another One Bites the Dust', previously performed in far better style by the group Queen. We both burst out laughing. What else was there to do? He, like me, was to be reduced to trooper within the next ten minutes. The sight of him in the NAAFI later that afternoon was the immediate cue for me to reciprocate his earlier serenade with a rendition of 'Yesterday', with apologies to Paul McCartney for my strained attempt.

During mid-1979 knowing whispers were busily relayed around the regiment that we were to be posted as a unit to Northern Ireland. It started in the wives' club, and soon after the commanding officer was told formally about the deployment. It is a strange and quaint military system, really, where the regimental wives have started packing their boxes to move and the soldiers of the regiment have not been properly informed of anything regarding the posting. Some days later we were gathered in the cinema in Hohne for a commanding officer's address. The rumours were correct. Omagh, County Tyrone, Northern Ireland, was to be work, rest and play for the next two years, from late 1980 till 1982, in an infantry role. What a bummer.

I knew nothing about Omagh other than that for soldiers it was considered to be a fairly safe posting, if there was such a thing in Northern Ireland. Families were to accompany the regiment on this two-year tour. It was bad enough for some of the blokes to face up to the prospect of the posting; for the wives and children who knew even less than us the next few months would be a very trying time. There were to be over six hundred shooting incidents, four hundred explosions and a total of over seventy deaths in 1980 alone. Of these deaths eight were soldiers, most of whom were based in the major cities of Belfast and Londonderry. However tragic and pointless their deaths were, it was more or less expected that someone would be killed during tours in these parts of the Province. We hoped for a better deal.

Throughout late 1979 and into 1980 the hunger strike was to manoeuvre itself into a higher media profile. Various requests were made for the so-called five demands to be granted to prisoners by high-ranking republican figures. It was a serious time in the Province, and we were due to arrive there right in the middle of the situation. The IRA had extended their murderous activities to include prison officers working at locations where republican prisoners were held, and during one of their attacks they had killed the wife of one of these men. Not exactly the type of news to be welcomed by wives of soldiers due to arrive in the Province within the next few weeks.

The demands being made by the prisoners were the right to wear their own clothes, the right to refuse to work, the right to associate with other prisoners, the right to recreation and education, and the right to their remission being restored. It was to be the hunger strike which was to dominate the two years of my time in the Province. The terrorist threat from the IRA still loomed, the killings were still going on, but in comparison with previous years the numbers of soldiers killed had decreased dramatically for some unknown reason.

My Northern Ireland training began. I was to be initiated into the art of being an infantry soldier, a different world from the one I had been used to over the previous few years. I had become accustomed to the 'cavalry' way of doing things, which was always a very comfortable way of dealing with life in the army, especially when we were away from camp on military exercises all over the country. Even on large NATO exercises in Germany it was not unknown for us to hide away our troop's armoured vehicles in large barns, leave one man on radio watch and another on guard stag, while the remainder of the troop would stroll into the local village and spend the evening in the local guest-house. They were always great places for some hot food and a few beers on cold winter nights.

Reality hit me straight between the eyes when we were all called, by troop, to the regimental quartermaster's department. I was issued with new patrol boots, which were higher than the normal issue we wore for work on the tank park. These gave the calf muscles extra support and they were a hell of a lot lighter and ideal for running in. We were given a new style of black padded gloves which were warm and comfortable, in complete contrast to the normal green woollen issue which some civil servant in the procurement department must have been given a serious backhander to take on as a job-lot from some supplier. These were just a few of the 'goodies' that were now on our signatures, and they were all welcome improvements. The other items of equipment we were given were the ones to set us thinking about the next few years ahead of us — riot helmets, flak jackets, extra first-field wound dressings and morphine ampoules.

Our training had begun.

Chapter 2

Northern Ireland: The First Time

F or me the beginning of August 1980 was a very trying time. I had transferred to the Royal Armoured Corps to start a new career that I hoped would culminate in commanding armoured vehicles on exercises in Germany, never really expecting to go to war, and reaping the benefits of duty-free living with perhaps the occasional trip to Canada and Cyprus thrown in for good measure. It never really dawned on me that I might have to go to Northern Ireland as an infantry-man. In all honesty the thought worried me, and I am sure I was not the only soldier involved in the training to have similar misgivings about our new role.

Sennelager, which was quite often referred to by British soldiers as 'the world's worst lager', was going to be our squadron home for the next two weeks. We were located at the somewhat cornily but aptly named training camp known as 'Fort-Nite', a name that some senior officer must have spent ages thinking up. Prior to the entire squadron deploying to this infantry training establishment we undertook our own internal troop training in the general area of Hohne Garrison, running around the place in heavy flak jackets and riot helmets, attending numerous lectures on the complexities of the Province, and generally pretending to know what we were doing in all matters relating to infantry patrol techniques and internal security measures.

Most of the internal security instruction carried out during this run-up phase was given by our own regimental instructors. The regiment itself had carried out a number of emergency tours in Northern Ireland as a complete unit, in 1974, when they were deployed to Londonderry for a four-month tour, and then again in 1976, this time covering the area around Armagh and East Tyrone. In between those duties and the impending two-year tour various troops had seen service in the Province, individually attached to a number of infantry battalions as part of our battle group commitment within 1BR Corps in Germany. Some of these troops had completed short tours in the city of Belfast some months previously, and were quite up to speed with the internal security tactics required and the generalities of what was going on in Northern Ireland. Most of the initial training we received was based on their experiences. There was also an NCO presence from one of the infantry regiments based in Celle, a large town only a short distance from our garrison. These guys were well up to date and were extremely good instructors who assisted enormously with our training in camp prior to us going on to Sennelager. Some of their older blokes had carried out eight or nine tours in the Province.

The initial training concentrated on the improvement of our general fitness. The physical training instructors had their hands full turning the 'fat tankies' into a bunch of Seb Coe racing snakes. Daily runs and gymnasium sessions became the order of the day, and we carried out extensive weapons handling with the 7.62 mm Self-Loading Rifle (SLR), which would be our personal weapon for the tour. First-aid lessons took on a more serious role, with particular attention being paid to the treatment of gunshot wounds and trauma. We also spent long periods practising a variety of other skills such as map reading and infantry patrol fire and movement, sessions held by both day and night. As we were an armoured reconnaissance regiment, map reading was second nature to the majority of us, the only difference being that it was now carried out on foot as opposed to on top of a Scimitar or Scorpion light tank. As someone who had transferred to the regiment with the intention of commanding tracked armoured vehicles, this new side to my army life came as a major culture shock, but I, along with my fellow cavalry soldiers, soon got the hang of it, and towards the latter part of the training I actually began to enjoy it, with only certain reservations.

We moved lock, stock and barrel as a squadron to the Northern Ireland Training and Tactics school at Sennelager to be greeted by a rather well-built, gruffly voiced infantry officer who was immediately christened 'Captain Chaos'. His *modus operandi*, along with his directing staff (DS), was to saturate us with criticism about all the bad drills we had carried out during the various internal security exercises and realistic scenarios, and on more than one occasion he insisted that most of the squadron would surely be wiped out by a terrorist attack 'en masse' if we were to carry out our patrolling techniques in the style we had acquired.

One of the more novel ways of debriefing he used was to run video recordings at the end of the day showing various members of the squadron in a multitude of highly embarrassing situations that they had been caught in during their day inside the training area. My troop sergeant and I had been caught by the short and curlies one day laying up in an observation post. We had been lying there slagging off the squadron leader in no uncertain terms. In the evening, just as the debrief was due to start, it became apparent exactly which video Captain Chaos was going to be playing to the attentive audience. The other guilty party and I just glanced at each other. I had a quick laugh to myself. After all, he was the senior rank and was likely to be in more shit than me, and luckily enough he had done most of the talking while the tape had been running. His face and neck went bright red in anticipation of the situation we were about to face. At the crucial point, where the barrage of our verbal abuse was just getting around to the question of the officer commanding's parenthood and the fact that we both assumed that his right hand was used more than his wife for sexual satisfaction, the video player broke down. Thank Christ for that. Lesson learnt again. If there is a video about, keep your trap well and truly shut.

My troop corporal had an equally embarrassing situation broadcast to the entire squadron the following evening, but gained a bit of respect back for the way in which he dealt with it. He had been involved in a scenario where a 'pretend' member of the public had approached him and had informed him that he believed there was a bomb in the street the patrol were in. The corporal concerned looked at his aide-mémoire and carried out the confirm, clear, cordon, control routine while the video rolled. Unfortunately for him he had done the clearing before the confirming and had established his incident control point in the doorway of a betting shop before finding out where the device was actually located. The video continued to roll. As the situation developed, Captain Chaos started talking to the NCO, asking him questions about the problem he had encountered and the actions he had taken. As the corporal knelt down, using an old jerry-can for support, and began to reel off a highly acceptable appraisal of the situation, Captain Chaos asked him if he had confirmed where the suspect device was located. With bluff and bluster, our troop corporal pointed up the street to the area of the baker's shop and with a fair degree of certainty explained that it was in the doorway some hundred metres away from the control point.

After Captain Chaos had milked the situation as far as he could, he told the bloke to look under his arse. There for all the world to see was a block of plastic explosive, a battery pack and the jerry-can of petrol. Steve, the troop corporal, looked at the smug face of the infantry captain and grinned while remarking on the fact that he had carried out this action purposely to test the observation skills of the younger soldiers in the troop and that they obviously had a lot of training to go through yet. As he walked away from the makeshift explosive device he sarcastically bollocked all the troopers for not picking him up on the mistake he had made to test them.

The exhaustive final exercise eventually came and went. The squadron had somehow managed to get through, and the next time we would be trogging around on patrol it would be in the Province for real. The thought of this really did nothing for me at all. I pined for the warmth and dryness of my tank turret.

In October 1980 my troop arrived in Lisanelly Barracks, which had been a British Army camp for years, situated on the northern outskirts of Omagh, County Tyrone. In the middle of the night we took over our accommodation from the outgoing regiment. The following day was spent having a multitude of intelligence briefs, updates on the movements of known or suspected terrorists and general orientation lectures on the area we were to cover. In total the regimental responsibility was to cover 784 square miles of the Province, including over fifty miles of the border areas with Eire. Along this border area there was in excess of thirty crossings points, of which only one was approved by the authorities; the others had all been cratered by explosives laid by the Royal Engineers to try to stop smuggling activities by the locals, and also to cause problems for terrorists looking for a quick getaway across to the South after they had carried out an attack. It was a joke. One day the illegal crossing would be impassable, the next day the locals would clear an area around the craters with their tractors or fill them in and carry on their routine as normal. My troop's area of responsibility covered quite a large area. In particular we had a patrol commitment to a small republican town about sixteen kilometres to the east of Omagh called Termon Rock, more commonly known as Carrickmore.

This little town harboured a hive of hardliners and was to take up more of our patrol time than anywhere else. It was to be the first place I had bricks thrown at me by the local schoolkids, the first place I saw a petrol bomb thrown, and the first place I witnessed a rubber bullet or baton gun being fired. Love at first sight, as they say. The locals made no bones about their support of the republican movement, which encouraged terrorism, and everyone who lived there despised us.

Exactly one year prior to our arrival the Provisional IRA had virtually sent an open invitation out to journalists, including a film crew from the *Panorama* television programme. The invitation was allegedly telephoned to their hotel in Eire, and informed them that if they wanted to see how the Provisionals were controlling republican areas they should go to Carrickmore. What the television team found was an organised patrol of black-hooded and heavily armed 'volunteers' from the Provisional IRA running their own illegal vehicle checkpoints in the area just outside the town in broad daylight. This was some distance away from the border areas, where this type of activity could be expected, and the whole escapade showed that the people we were likely to be up against were in no way afraid to show their strength in public, and in the worst-case scenario they would obviously be prepared to take us on face to face if they so wished. These were professional, dedicated and capable soldiers.

Life in the Province somehow went on as usual. Daily patrols became normal and there was even a decent social life. Omagh was considered to be a fairly safe place for a regimental two-year residential tour. The married soldiers' wives took shopping trips to Belfast and other large towns and cities, their kids went to schools in the local town, and we had free access to a wide range of pubs and clubs. A number of the lads played sports for the local rugby and hockey teams. This fraternisation did not extend to the Gaelic football or hurley teams, though. There was still a line to be drawn. The only major threat came from the local Ulster Defence Regiment (UDR), whose younger male members were not too enthralled with the way their female population tended to ignore with some vigour their protestations about going off with 'the Brits'. Fights in certain nightclubs in the town were commonplace. It was just like being back in Hohne again.

One Friday evening I was just lazing about in the accommodation block, doing nothing in particular, thinking about that night's possible entertainment in town, when I was disturbed by my troop sergeant, a friend of mine. He came up to me and asked whether I would mind helping out with the manpower required for the Quick Reaction Force (QRF). The duty of the force was to be on stand-by for any situation requiring extra manpower, to support troops on the ground and to react to incidents anywhere within our regiment's area of responsibility. Every troop took its turn to complete a twenty-four-hour period, which mainly consisted of watching videos and sleeping until there was a call from the operations room to go out to an incident or to carry out a patrol in a particular area. The QRF on duty that day was short of a bloke for a routine helicopter patrol around the Carrickmore area, and the operations room had demanded a presence in the air over what used to be the old rectory, now a burnt-out shell of a building. This type of operation was usually referred to as 'top cover', and was meant to act as a deterrent to any possible terrorist attack being considered by active service unit volunteers. In hot pursuit a helicopter is an extremely useful vehicle for tracking and following suspects, by both day and night.

It was my Friday off, the first one for ages, and I politely told him to fuck off. After a bit of bartering he told me that if I did him this favour I could pick any extra day off I wished the following week. It seemed like a pretty good idea to agree at the time, as the helicopter patrol was only likely to last a few hours and they were good fun anyway. I could still be back in camp before the pubs shut. I agreed. I made my way to the armoury and picked up my SLR, then I walked back across the helicopter landing pad to the troop's accommodation and got my webbing and combat uniform sorted out, gave my rifle a quick clean and oiled the working parts, then it was down to the loading bay where a twenty-round magazine was fitted ready for the patrol. There were to be four of us in the chopper, a Scout, with two men sat each side, facing out, with our legs dangling over the skids. We knelt down in pairs facing the cockpit of the Scout as the pilot finished his pre-flight checks, and after he had checked that his hair was looking good and had put on his Ray-Ban sunglasses, he gave us the thumbs-up. We dashed over to the helicopter, ducking as we approached the blades circling above our heads. The Scout lifted off, banked over towards the north, and then headed east towards Carrickmore. There was always a buzz to be had from this type of patrolling – the adrenalin rush as the helicopter banks over is a great experience. If it could be bottled and sold you could make a small fortune.

As we flew out of the Lisanelly Barracks area and headed away from camp I noticed a greater number of Royal Ulster Constabulary (RUC) Land Rover patrols than usual moving along the road. In addition it struck me that they appeared to be escorting a large number of transporter-sized container trucks, all heading along the Drumnakilly road away from the town. As well as these ground vehicles and foot patrols we were joined in the air by a number of other helicopters, a mixture of Wessex, Lynx and other Scouts, all generally moving towards the east. I wondered what the hell was going on. I had the feeling I had been mugged into something that was going to last more than a few hours. It was a bit like a scene from the film *Apocalypse Now*; if some loudspeakers had burst into life with Wagner's 'Ride of the Valkyries' the scene would have been set to perfection.

The convoy turned out to be the construction teams and their escorts moving into Carrickmore to set up the new police station, which was to be located where the remains of the old rectory were. We were part of the operation to give top cover to the whole show, or at least that's how it appeared to me. I was sadly mistaken. On the way there we were told over the radio to deploy on the ground at the old rectory and meet up with other call signs from our regiment who were already in position. As we jumped off the Scout skids, members of our regiment's close observation troop took our places. They had been laying out at the rectory for a number of weeks, watching and securing the area, and were being relieved by us. As we changed over there was an exchange of the usual abusive banter, with them having the upper hand. As we covered their departure from the area their grins were certainly wider than ours.

We moved into the stables at the old rectory and set up our mini-cookers for a brew. We had no formal instructions for our deployment. Obviously the operations room back in Omagh had cuffed it a little bit by telling us to land, and I did not think they really knew what to do with us now that we were there. There were enough police and troops around the place to start a mini-war, and so we thought if we kept out of sight and pretended to know what we were doing no one would bother us, and then we could catch the next helicopter back to camp. Unfortunately this was not to be the case. All we had with us were belt kits consisting of the bare essentials for either a short, or at the most an overnight, patrol; no sleeping bags, no rations, just ammunition and brew kits with a snack-pack of biscuits and a few chocolate bars.

Billy, my troop sergeant, came back from the swiftly set up operations room and with rather a red face asked if we were all fine and enjoying ourselves; had we had a brew? The stables were quite good, weren't they? His questions showed a concern for our welfare previously unseen. I looked at him with a sly grin and asked the question on behalf of the other blokes in the troop. 'Bill, get to the point. What the fuck is going on here?' He replied that the operations room had informed him that we were to perform the task of base security for the new complex. We would carry out the anti-mortar baseplate patrols, man the operations room, carry out liaison with military and police search teams and general patrolling in the immediate area – all this on a packet of biscuits and a bar of chocolate! Six weeks later we headed back to camp. Six fucking weeks of Carrickmore! Believe you me, I was more than ready to go back to Omagh.

The weeks spent at Carrickmore on our prolonged visit actually turned out to be quite a good laugh on one or two occasions. One of these highlights was one evening when 2nd Troop from my squadron was tasked with the security of a grand country house at Termon, on the outskirts of the village, belonging to a retired British Army officer. The owner was out of the country at the time. The retired colonel and his family had been there for years and had surprisingly remained untouched by the Troubles. However, because of the overnight arrival of a police station in the area, and the possibility of various backlashes by the local community, it was decided to provide cover and protection to this location, among a number of others. Second Troop were hiding up in the house during the day and then putting lads out in observation positions with night viewing aids during the hours of dark to defend the house against any attacks.

We decided to pay them a courtesy visit one evening while we were on a routine patrol, and informed them of our imminent arrival on the radio just as we were about a hundred metres away. As I spoke to their radio operator I could hear shrieks of laughter in the background. Billy and I looked at each other with some confusion as their radio operator, who was laughing hysterically as he spoke to me, told us to approach from the south as they had laid out trip flares on all routes in to the house except from that direction. On entering the house it became apparent what they were all laughing about. One of the lads in the troop had been into the cellar of the house and had located a few bottles of the retired colonel's vintage port and claret; other members had found a wardrobe upstairs containing a stack of old colonial-style uniforms, ball gowns, wigs and hats. The scene that lay before us was hilarious, the complete troop in fancy dress drinking port and toasting the regiment. Captain Chaos would surely have burst a blood vessel.

Overall our tour in Omagh had been relatively quiet. We had been involved in a few minor scraps in Strabane and Carrickmore during the hunger strike period, but nothing compared to what various infantry battalions had been putting up with in Londonderry and Belfast over the same period. Those lads really had been earning their extra pay.

We were patrolling through Strabane one afternoon when two 'Molotov cocktails' came flying at us from behind a six-foot wall on the 'Head of Town' estate. As the milk bottles smashed the inflammable contents immediately spread, and with a loud whooshing noise nearly caught two of our lads who were at the rear of the patrol. As myself and a colleague legged it up the alleyway in pursuit of the missile throwers we were met by a hail of bricks and bottles. We had not had time to put our riot helmets on and Steve, my mate in the chase, took half a house brick straight in the face. Blood started to gush from his eyelid, and we halted on the corner in a doorway facing on to the playground where a gang of about fifty or so teenagers and kids had gathered, ready for us to come into sight. They hurled abuse at us, baiting us to come out in the open. They suddenly bomb-burst in all directions. It was sometimes a ploy among terrorists in the Province to use kids as shields for a shooting. The kids would be given a signal and spread, the terrorist would take a few shots at the army patrol, and then the kids would converge again, blocking any return of fire. This time, however, the bomb burst was due to the rest of our patrol. They had radioed to our two Land Rovers, which had been carrying out a satellite patrol around the area where we were on foot. The two Land Rovers sped across the playground, chasing the teenagers – it was quite exciting to watch. As the vehicles pursued the kids they shot off in all directions. One made the mistake of running straight into the alleyway where Steve and I were waiting, and when he was about ten feet away Steve launched the half-brick at him. It caught him in the forehead and he yelled, screamed, 'You fucking bastards,' and legged it off in the opposite direction. Steve turned to me and laughed out loud, and with obvious satisfaction said, 'That'll teach the little bastard.'

The blood on Steve's face was now looking quite dramatic, and as the Land Rovers had completed their chase we were picked up and taken back to our base. Steve was taken in to see the duty medic who, after cleaning up the mess on his forehead, told him that a few clips were all that were needed. It looked a lot worse than it actually was because of the great amount of blood that had spread all over the place. The medic told Steve that he would get no compensation for it, though; that was for stitches only. Steve proceeded to tell the medic that if he did not put the stitches in he would be needing some himself, so two stitches and a claim for a few hundred pounds later Steve was happy. News of the compensation spread like wildfire, and from then on everyone tried to catch a brick. Billy drew the line and demanded that in future everyone would wear helmets at all times; he was not going to have our troop claiming for injuries left, right and centre.

Our troop had a number of minor successes, one of which consisted of an arms find in the area of Hadden's Quarry, just on the outskirts of Carrickmore. We had split into two sections and our section had decided to take a break in the cover of some shrub only a few yards away from the quarry but about a hundred yards away from the main road. As we gathered around to have our tea break, Billy told one of the lads to move about fifty yards further up the hill and keep watch. The bloke concerned took the general-purpose machinegun with him and sauntered off. A few minutes later he returned, and Billy asked him what the fuck he thought he was playing at, to which the guy sarcastically responded that he had found a bag of weapons. Billy told him that he should stop playing the prat and fuck off back up the hill. The bloke turned, shrugged his shoulders, huffed a bit, and walked off. Within a few minutes he was back again with a big grin on his face. He looked at Billy and quite smugly stated that there were five of them. Billy looked at me and told me to go and have a look to see what was there, and if the lad concerned was waffling I had his full permission to give him a dig. We slowly moved up the hill, and the lad pointed out an area of thicker bushes where I should look. Sure enough, there was a large plastic bag about four foot in length with a carry strap tied at both ends leaving a sling in the middle. The contents could easily be carried over the shoulder with the sling. As I was just about to tell Billy to come and have a look the lad who had found the package cut through the plastic with his machete. I could see what was obviously the barrel of some sort of rifle. I looked at him straight in the eye and told him that he was a complete tosser and not to touch the package again. I would rather go home that evening with a full set of arms and legs.

The troop leader was called on the radio and told to join us at the quarry; his half of the patrol were about half a mile away. When he arrived he was fully briefed on the situation and told about the arms find that had been uncovered. Like most young troop leaders he was highly excitable, and came out with a number of options on how the find should be dealt with. He was a cracking bloke but sometimes needed Billy's experience to guide him in the right direction. There was only one course of action and that was to bring out the experts to have a look at the contents and leave every decision to them. Within an hour or so the Ordnance Corps bomb disposal officer and his team that dealt with these situations had arrived. The search adviser from the Royal Engineers had been the first bloke to walk up to the find and do his particular business. He came back to us after about half an hour and reported that he had dealt with the possibility of the package being booby-trapped.

The bloke who had slit the pack open looked at me and Billy and made a loud swallowing noise in his throat. His actions earlier could have cost us dearly if the package had been connected to an explosive device. This had been drummed into us time and time again at Sennelager during our training before deployment. There was no point on dwelling on the subject — he knew what he had done, and that was enough.

The contents of the bag were made safe and put on display. They consisted of a 7mm SAFN, a .303 Springfield, a .303 SMLE, a Lee Enfield and a Thompson submachine-gun. In addition to the weapons there were several magazines appropriate to the find and a mixture of ammunition. The weapons were well greased and wrapped in newspaper within the plastic covering. We headed back to our troop store in camp and the troop leader appeared later with a case of beer. There were five weapons not available to the Provisionals any more.

As our party progressed into the small hours we encouraged the troop leader to kick the arse right out of his mess bill and lay on some champagne for the boys. Being the good lad that he was, he agreed that he should as well. He was the typical short-term commissioned officer, probably in for three years as part of a deal with his family, like so many other young officers in the regiment whose careers had been moulded for them from the time they were toddlers. Boarding school, the army, the family business. This particular troop leader and I were quite friendly. He had a really good sense of humour, and was always ready with a fast, witty reply to most situations, which, considering the company he kept, he needed. We were having a chat one afternoon during a patrol and he said that I should instruct the lads to move off the road and into cover for a lunch break. As we both searched around in the kidney pouches of our webbing to see what delights the Army Catering Corps had put together for us, he suddenly turned and asked me if I would like a glass of wine. This was Carrickmore, we were conducting a patrol in a dangerous area of Northern Ireland, and so while the rest of the Province carried out its patrols rigidly and by the book, we had a glass or two of Cabernet Sauvignon with our packed lunch, as only the cavalry would. He asked me if I had any plans for my future in the army, and quite honestly I told him that I figured if I was quick enough in getting my lance-corporal ranking back again I would probably like to make a full-term career of it, and possibly end up becoming a warrant officer and ultimately be commissioned from the ranks. I asked him the same question. He sipped his wine, rubbed his chin and very seriously said that he would be quite happy if he could make lieutenant. He then grinned and said that he doubted he would get that far! He actually left as a captain, and so surpassed his own expectations.

The hunger strikes were in full swing, and over this period ten republican prisoners were to starve themselves to death, becoming martyrs for their cause. Bobby Sands, because of his political position, as MP for Fermanagh and South Tyrone was probably the most celebrated of the hunger strikers, and it was expected that the shit would hit the fan when he died. By the end of April 1981 he had been on his strike for close on sixty days; he was not expected to last much longer. We had been deployed to Clogher in support of another squadron from our regiment; the general idea was that we would mount observation posts along the border areas as attacks on military installations were expected the moment that news of Sands's demise was released. The plan was that we could intercept any terrorists making their way back across the border after any such attacks had taken place, or possibly pre-empt them and stop any crossing into the North by the illegal crossing points. We settled into our positions for some long cold nights. The rain soaked us and it was a pretty dismal time. During the late evening on 5 May the operations officer at Clogher came on the radio. 'All call signs be aware that Bravo Sierra [Sands] has left this location for higher echelons. Over.' All the observation-post radio operators acknowledged the transmission; it was now time to watch our fronts.

The rain had subsided and there was a definite chill in the air. The clouds had parted and I could make out the stars beginning to peek through. It was extremely quiet and cold. Bang! There was a huge explosion somewhere to our south, possibly about ten kilometres away; it was definitely in the Republic. One of the call signs at the most southern part of the physical feature we were covering sent a 'contact' report. This consisted of an appraisal of where they thought the explosion was, and after the operator had finished speaking the operations room asked all the various posts for their estimations on the same explosion. In turn each call sign came up on the radio and gave its appraisal. One call sign had not answered, and for a full ten minutes the operations officer was calling them for a reply. Eventually a sleepy, muffled, murmuring Liverpudlian accent answered one of the checks. The operations officer asked for a contact report on the explosion. After about two minutes' deathly silence the same Scouse accent came back with the response, 'Er, wor explosion's that, like? Over.' From that day forward the person concerned was christened 'Tommy', as in the deaf, dumb and blind kid.

Carrickmore always appeared to be quiet. Only once in a while would we come under pressure on patrol, usually from the kids leaving school in the afternoon. They would hurl abuse at us as we walked down the road, and if we were feeling in the mood we would bait them – it was always good fun. After the various insults had been exchanged and maybe the odd brick thrown everybody would lose interest and stroll away, the kids to their homes and us back to the police station. For a notorious village like this, with its alleged support for the republican cause, it was almost subdued most of the time. That was until Easter arrived, when the republican emotions of the local population took priority over normal life. Carrickmore came into its own at Easter, as I was to see for myself. I was part of a patrol tasked to stay a few hundred yards away from the martyrs' remembrance garden just on the outskirts of the village. I honestly expected to see a few hundred people attend the rally at the most. At about half past three that afternoon we heard the sounds of drums coming from the centre of the village as a procession made its way towards the site. At the head of the parade were fourteen men dressed in camouflage jackets, green trousers, black berets and masks. The front few marchers carried a selection of flags, including the starry plough, the Fianna flag and the inevitable Tricolour. The procession gathered at the remembrance garden. By now the crowd had swelled to about three thousand, quite a sight for this place. A speech was given by James Gibney, a high-ranking Sinn Fein official who was instrumental in making Bobby Sands the parliamentary candidate and eventual Member for Fermanagh and South Tyrone. Then, towards the end of the rally, a masked person from the colour party moved forward to the rostrum and made a statement on behalf of the Provisional Army Council. He was flanked on either side by other masked men; they both held handguns but fired no shots. The information from our observation point was transmitted to our operations room, and they confirmed that we were to stand off and observe only; there was to be no attempt to recover the weapons. No fun and games that afternoon.

The parade dispersed, and after helping the RUC to get the traffic moving away from the area as quickly as possible we returned to the police station, which had by now become our second home. As we made our way to the canteen we were informed of another task we were to carry out later that afternoon. Two members of our Close Observation Troop (COT) had been in cover extremely close to the procession and would need to tag on to the end of one of our patrols to return to the police station undetected. They had been a few feet away from the edge of the crowd and had taken some photographs of the gun-bearers which were required for scrutiny by Special Branch on their return. Later that week two men from the local area were arrested and two handguns were recovered. A good result from our regiment's covert activities.

What I did discover during this period was the presence of a few specialised covert units operating in the Province. I had obviously heard of the Special Air Service (SAS) – their historic embassy siege at Princes Gate had taken place in May 1980 and had blown the anonymity they had managed to retain for many years. I had just walked back into my room in Hohne at about 7.30 p.m. from a late tea after rugby training to see the now famous balcony scenes transmitted live from Kensington. These men became the instant heroes of virtually every soldier in the British Army, myself included.

I knew the SAS was in the Province, but what they did and where they were located was only to become fully apparent some years later. My first and only contact with them during my two years in Omagh came about one evening while my troop was on QRF in camp. Billy, our troop sergeant, had been called over to the operations room for a briefing, and as he left we all kitted up ready for a potential crash-out. There was a call on the Tannoy in the QRF room for us all to go across to the regimental intelligence cell. As our section entered the room I noticed a guy in lightweight combats, wearing an open baggy combat smock. At his side lay a rucksack with a large 'Westminster' radio inside. He had an earpiece running to the Bergen and he was speaking in whispered tones into the small microphone unit. His hair was slightly longer than a normal soldier's, and leaning against his Bergen (backpack) was a foreign rifle, a Heckler and Koch HK53. As he leaned forward to stand up I also noticed a holster containing what appeared to be a Browning pistol inside his smock. Fucking hell, he was one of them, and we were actually going to chat to him!

The briefing he gave was very short and basically consisted of him telling us that if an operation taking place in our immediate area was in need of a cordon, we were it. The cordon supplied by our men would give the required protection for his team to be extracted from the area covertly, and would stop any civilians going into the incident area before the police were called in. We would get any further instructions should we be deployed. We were not informed of what kind of operation they were carrying out, or where it was being instigated. About twenty minutes later he whispered something into the small microphone, then stood up and said, 'Thanks very much, gents, that's it. Sorry to have interrupted your evening,' and then left the room. Those twenty minutes had intrigued me. I had just turned twenty-one and had not even considered my future outside the turret of an armoured vehicle. That evening planted the seed for the future. Although I had no plans to join the SAS, it did occur to me that there might be close alternatives whose roles I was not fully aware of.

Many of my own regiment's COT were always making noises about a unit that they referred to as 'Fourteen', and had been involved in carrying out tasks for the Tasking Co-ordination Group (TCG). I knew this particular set-up controlled the various covert operations within the Province, and also deployed the COTs for long-term surveillance tasks. Our COT lads had made various drawn-out references to how they had done this job for 'Fourteen' and that job for 'Fourteen'. Once again, as with the SAS, this mystical bunch of people intrigued me, and I had the vague notion that it might be something I would like to find out more about.

I had walked into the 'choggie' shop in the camp one evening to grab a burger. This shop was like a greasy-spoon café run by Asian people whose families had served the British Army for years. In the old days they did it as servants; these days they did it for vast profits, and most drove around in top-of-the-range Mercedes and BMWs. In front of me was a familiar face. I knew he was another soldier, only he had long hair and was wearing scruffy civilian clothes. I recalled that he was a lad who had been a few years senior to me at the Apprentice College at Chepstow. We had played rugby together. He recognised me straight away, and we shook hands and sat down for a brew and a chat. I asked him what he was up to and what was he doing here dressed like that. He evaded the questions with a hint of embarrassment, but the more he evaded the more I persisted. I asked him directly whether he was involved with this 'Fourteen' bunch, and at this he appeared to get a little shirty and asked me what I knew about them. I innocently replied that I did not really know that much, but I was all ears if he had anything to tell me. He made a pretty feeble excuse for leaving after about ten minutes, but he told me that if I was really interested to keep an eye on normal regimental routine orders for a reference to 'Special Duties'.

After two years our tour in Omagh eventually came to an end and we prepared to move to England after handing over to the incoming regiment. We were lucky enough to leave the Province without any loss of life; others had not been so fortunate. During our two-year tour there had been over 2,000 shooting incidents within the Province, just over 1,000 explosions, and over 270 deaths, of which 39 had been regular soldiers.

We were to be posted to Carver Barracks, just outside the town of Saffron Walden in Essex. We were to be redeployed as a light armoured reconnaissance unit equipped once again with Scimitars. Home at last.

The two-year tour in Omagh had instilled in me more than a passing interest in these 'covert' units I had heard about, and the sense of intrigue was still there a few years later. A number of the lads who were in our COT had tried selection for these duties. One or two had been successful, but the majority had been refused and had returned to regimental life. The failure rate was high, and some very competent guys I knew had been returned for one reason or another. I had completed an exchange visit to an Italian armoured unit, which was probably the worst jaunt I had ever been on, and I had attended and passed my Royal Armoured Corps crew commander's course, which in sharp contrast to the 'Italian Job' was probably the best course I had been involved in since I joined the army. A six-month tour of Cyprus as part of the United Nations scout car squadron was under my belt, and life seemed to be heading in one direction – towards regimental duty. The way things were going it was likely that at best I would end up as a warrant officer within my own regiment. Nothing wrong with that other than I was not totally convinced it was what I wanted. I was twenty-six years old, a corporal, and looking for something other than normal soldiering.

I had read regimental orders one evening and, lo and behold, a section contained within the orders asked for volunteers to attend selection for arduous training with a view to being considered for Special Duties. Candidates were to contact the adjutant or chief clerk for more details. I decided that I would pay the chief clerk's office a visit the next day.

Chapter 3

Fourteen Selection

After our routine squadron parade on the Wednesday morning I had made my way into our tank hangar. I offered some pathetic excuse to my troop sergeant about needing to see the chief clerk about travel warrant claims and sneaked back out of the hangar. I made my way from the tank park, which was at the far end of camp, to the regimental headquarters. The corridor of this building was quite a daunting place, filled with various pieces of memorabilia depicting the long and distinguished history of the regiment. A track record was displayed along its walls of over three hundred years of campaigns in which the regiment had been involved. It was quite a sight — an awesome history of bloody cavalry warfare including the Boyne, Blenheim, Waterloo and the Zulu wars of the late 1870s. I had only ventured into this building previously when it was absolutely necessary, usually if I had been in trouble. It contained the offices of the RSM, the adjutant and the commanding officer, very much hallowed ground and not the kind of place for junior ranks to be wandering around aimlessly. With this in mind, I quickly made my way through the oak-panelled entrance and swiftly moved along the highly polished corridor to the chief clerk's office in the hope that I would not be spotted by anyone from the hierarchy who might start asking awkward questions.

The chief clerk was a bloke from Newport with an extremely high-pitched voice. He was known by everyone in the regiment as 'Screechy', and so, rather predictably, after I had knocked on his door, this shrieking voice called out and asked what I wanted. I moved forward to Screechy's desk and asked him if I could have a personal chat concerning the article I had seen on regimental routine orders about Special Duties.

What happened next amused the hell out of me. Picture the scene – a super-efficient chief clerk stood up, strained his neck and looked over my shoulder to check that there was no one behind me at the door listening to our conversation. He then literally jumped up from behind his desk and moved quickly to his office door, then looked up and down the corridor, checked there was no one around, and called to his orderly room corporal that he was not to be disturbed under any circumstances. He came back into the room and told me to take a seat, then leaned over his desk and beckoned me to lean forward. I thought for one minute he was going to kiss me. It reminded me of one of the television programmes with Griff Rhys Jones and Mel Smith having one of their close-up face-to-face conversations.

'Well, Corporal Lewis, this is a turn-up for the books,' he said. 'Have you really thought about this?'

'Yes, sir, I have,' I replied.

'In which case, young man, I admire you and I will help you.'

The sound of this choirboy voice screeching at me nearly had me bursting out laughing, but I could not fault the bloke. He was being extremely genuine. He was also a very powerful character within the regiment whom I needed on my side – I had to listen to what he was saying. He asked me which particular special duties unit I was interested in. I told him I didn't realise there was that much of a choice. He then listed two or three specialist courses within the services that I was eligible to have a go at, and mentioned one that, because I was a junior rank, would not accept me.

I asked him which one was the 'Fourteen Int. Company' course, and once again he squeaked out his reply, informing me that this was the Special Duties section applicable to the covert surveillance unit that had specific responsibility for Northern Ireland – this time the squeak was whispered. He then proceeded to tell me the ins and outs of how he could help me apply, and told me to follow him out of his office up the corridor of power. It was like a scene from any one of the Peter Sellers Pink Panther movies, with Screechy creeping up the corridor looking back at me and giving me the thumbs-up. I was half expecting an oriental karate expert named Cato to jump from the skylight to test my reactions, and all this was happening in the regimental headquarters corridor.

As we made our covert approach to the adjutant's office, the first face I saw was that of my own squadron leader, a mumbling, punch-drunk major known within the regiment as Toddy. It was very unusual for a junior rank, especially me, to be walking about in RHQ with the chief clerk, and Toddy looked at me and mumbled some sort of question. I clearly said 'Pardon, sir?' in reply. Toddy mumbled some kind of question again. A little louder and more clearly I once again said 'Pardon, sir?', knowing full well it would annoy him not to know why I was in RHQ. He gave me a dirty look and I thought I heard him mumble something like 'Fuck it' as he walked off down the corridor, leaving me with the chief clerk outside the adjutant's office.

Screechy indicated for me to stand just to the right of the adjutant's door and to hang on there while he had a quick chat with the man, so for two minutes I stood in the corridor waiting for Cato to leap out on me. Screechy then popped his head around the door and 'smuggled' me in. This was getting more and more like a comedy sketch by the minute.

The adjutant asked me the same sort of questions as the chief clerk had, and during our conversation went over to what they termed the 'war safe', brought out a file named Operation Peregrine, and proceeded to go through various directives contained within the instructions which were to be given to anyone who had applied for this particular selection process. One of the prerequisites of attending the course was a commanding officer's interview. The adjutant said that he had better have a quick chat with the commanding officer and see if he could get me in to see him there and then. This was all happening with increasing rapidity. First the chief clerk, then the adjutant, and now the Old Man himself. I had only gone in for a quick fact-finding chat.

I was dressed in tank-park denims, beret and belt, and was extremely greasy and dirty, having just been in the middle of a service on my Scimitar light armoured tank when I decided to have a skive and a chat with Screechy about my possible application. To be put in front of the commanding officer in this manner was very unusual, to say the least. However, the CO was a superb bloke whom I knew very well. I had been his driver for a brief period a few years previously. He was a fanatical country sportsman who excelled at fly-fishing and deerstalking. He was aware of my passion for fishing – we had spent a few days together fishing in the Inter-Services Fly-Fishing Championships in Rutland earlier the same year. He was the epitome of what you would call a 'soldier's officer', but was also an extremely hard bloke, who in his younger days had not been backward when it came to giving someone a clip across the ear. Funnily enough he had threatened to give me a filling-in one morning when I had annoyed him over something trivial, but he was a big enough man to apologise to me minutes later, though directly after the apology he told me to get my fags out. Apparently his wife had been really bugging him about giving up smoking and had thrown his packet of cigarettes away, and I just happened to be the first person he saw next. After a personal interview that lasted about half an hour he endorsed my application, the required paperwork was fully completed, and I was told to wait for a date for my initial interview. Time to start training.

My squadron sergeant-major was quite a good bloke, with whom I had got along well; he had also been a bit of a tearaway in his younger days. He was the only bloke I knew who had five clasps on his General Service Medal for various campaigns he had been involved in, but no Long Service and Good Conduct gong to go with it. My hero! Generally he was very on-side when I told him what I was thinking of doing. He said that he would be happy to let me carry out my personal training during working hours, and if I needed help with anything he would point me in the right direction. So far, so good. He did say that I ought to let the squadron leader know my intentions, and as there was no time like the present I followed him into Toddy's office. Toddy then proceeded to tell me that he had tried the same course some time ago when he had been a subaltern, and that he had been found unsuitable. He glanced at me with a complete look of disdain and asked if I knew what he meant. I said, 'What, you mean you failed, sir?' He looked at me again and said quite sharply that no, he had not failed, he was found to be 'unsuitable', and he would expect the same to happen to me. If anything was going to reinforce my determination to pass, it was this twat. The chief clerk called me to his office and informed me that another of my mates had been in to see him and was trying for the same selection, and that maybe we ought to get together for training. It happened to be an extremely close friend of mine, Ian 'Buttocks' Edwards, who, like me, had kept his application quiet. He was one of our clique of about eight trusted and tested mates within the regiment. He was extremely fit, although his beer gut and large buttocks sometimes gave a false impression of this hidden fitness. Together, and with some assistance from one or two of the gymnasium and training wing staff, we embarked upon our training schedule – weapons handling on the SLR and 9mm Browning pistol, weight training, map reading, sprints, distance running, orienteering and the odd spell of Kim's game to improve our memory retention. Basically this requires having to memorise a number of objects placed on a table which you are allowed to look at for a given time, then you look away from the table and try to recall what objects you saw. After a while this method trains your brain to remember in far greater detail everyday occurrences that you would normally dismiss – car registrations, people's clothing and visible distinguishing features, along with their activities, become clearly recollected. We became very proficient at all the required skills.

My biggest problem was distance running. I could quite happily play a decent game of rugby and I could swim very well, but when it came to basic fitness running tests I was completely useless, and I invariably just managed to scrape through in the allotted time requirement for my age group. This would not be good enough for the tests I was likely to be undertaking. Running the basic fitness test became a twice-daily necessity, along with all the other training. Ian and I pushed and encouraged each other all the way. My times for the runs came down from just over thirteen minutes to just under ten minutes in the space of a few weeks. It felt good, but by God it hurt.

I was required to attend a one-day interview in Bovington, Dorset. I had been to Bovington many times and had spent three months there previously on my crew commander's course, so knew the place very well. This interview consisted of a test day covering, luckily enough, all the things Ian and I had been practising over the previous few weeks. We were put through our paces on fitness, weapons handling and map reading; they also threw in one or two mental agility tests for good measure. One of these tests apparently gives the interviewers an insight into the mental state of the applicant and consists of some strange questions to be answered in rapid time. I knew that I had done well at all the other tests, but maybe I was a nutcase! We were also interviewed by the 'panel of three', the first time I had undertaken this type of routine. One of the panel was an extremely convivial character who directed his questions at me in a very sociable way. His sidekick was an obnoxious, ignorant block whose questions were asked in a very demanding and demeaning tone. The third bloke just sat there, saying nothing and taking notes. Mr Nice asked me what kind of car I drove. At the time it was an Escort XR3i. He commented that they were quite nice cars and probably quick off the mark. Mr Nasty immediately jumped in with the comment that I must be a 'flash fucker' who fancied his chances at being a racing driver. They continued the double act, with Mr Nice observing the fact that I had a front tooth missing, the result of a timely placed kick to the face during a game of rugby. I explained this. Mr Nasty, in his usual form of attack, accused me of being a troublemaker and added that I had probably had the tooth knocked out by some irate husband who had caught me with his wife. The 'interview' closed after about half an hour, and I was asked to wait in the corridor. After ten minutes I was called back in. I was told that they considered me to be suitable for progressing to the next stage in the process. This was what the interviewer called 'Pre-Camp One'. We would be notified of our start date for this in due course. I was given some paperwork to take back to my unit and dismissed. Mr Nasty grinned and said 'Well done' in an unconvincing way as I nodded and thanked all three for their time. I had the feeling I would be seeing him again some time.

Pre-camp One was held in Sutton Coldfield. I had been there once many years before for three days, just before I joined the army. It was where young recruits were administered and given basic tests prior to being launched into their careers. It felt strange to be back there again after all these years.

The pre-camp session was a fairly formal period of three days where all the potential recruits for the Special Duties course gathered. They were from all three services and made up of male and female applicants. We were all numbered off and were given a series of briefings on how we should not divulge details of our backgrounds or services to any other candidate, and not discuss any personal matters with anyone other than the directing staff (DS). There were two people from my own regiment who were part of the staff – one was a senior rank who had disappeared from regimental duties some years previously and the other a clerk. At my initial interview the clerk had smiled at me and made some quip about being very surprised to see Ian and me attending this course. I ignored him. I did not know where his loyalties lay, and I was not about to put them to the test within the first hour of arriving there.

The three days involved us being brought up to speed on basic infantry patrol techniques, map reading, weapons handling and fitness training. The idea was to have all the students, no matter what their backgrounds, arriving at the next stage on an even keel, whether they were a leading seaman, a nurse or a paratrooper. Incredibly, even after day one some of the students started to drop out. This was the pre-test stage, for fuck's sake. Did they expect to get issued their cloak and dagger and sent behind enemy lines by the end of the day? The pre-camp stage came to an end on the lunch-time of the third day, and we were told to parade by our groups on the drill square and await the arrival of the coaches.

The luxury coaches duly arrived and we were all given a packed lunch containing a few sandwiches, a drink and a Mars bar, and then we were sent on our way. The coaches headed off towards the M5, then further west into the Worcestershire and Gloucestershire border areas. As we headed into the Welsh borders I looked out of the coach window at the mountainous area looming in the distance. I immediately knew that the next few days were going to be hard going. We eventually arrived at a training camp used mostly by territorial soldiers and cadets on adventure training exercises.

Everything seemed quite peaceful. It was a beautiful sunny day and the light wisps of clouds gathering over the mountains showed no signs of breaking into rain. The coach pulled in beside one of the accommodation blocks and one of the Pre-Camp One DS at the front of the coach shouted for us all to remain in our seats while he went and checked that our accommodation was ready for us.

Crash! Bang! Wallop! What appeared next resembled a mass of frothing, raging madmen. They rampaged into the coach, while more were waiting outside – a deluge of Royal Marines Commando 'Green Berets' and an equal number of Parachute Regiment 'Red Berets' appeared from every angle. Ranting, screaming and shouting like crazy, this wave of hate shouted abuse at us as we ran from the coach: 'Get in the fucking block, you piece of shit', 'Carry your fucking case above your head, you wanker', 'Run faster, you fucking cretin', 'Who are you fucking looking at, you worthless heap of crap?' The final shout as we ran like scared rabbits into the block was 'Outside, two minutes, boots, lightweights and red PT top. Now, fucking move it'. The next ten days or so saw me being run ragged, shouted at, abused mentally, and generally fucked about from arsehole to breakfast, as they say. This was 'Camp One'.

The whole point of Camp One was to weed out the recruits who were along just for the ride, and to test the ability of potential candidates to work under pressure while physically and mentally knackered. It certainly did that. If my memory serves me correctly the total number on my course who had started at Pre-Camp One was about 200. There were about 150 of us on the coaches to Camp One, and by the end of the first two days there were about another 50 who had jacked their hands in. I thought of Toddy, and his comments about me probably not getting through the selection. As far as I was concerned I was not going anywhere. If I was leaving, it would be either through the DS telling me to go or through injury.

The first item on the agenda was the basic fitness test, a run and walk over a distance of one and a half miles immediately followed by a straight run back to the finish, returning along the same route. The run was against the clock, and every candidate had to get back to the finish within eleven and a half minutes. My training had paid off and I passed the line in just under nine and a half minutes. I had decided to stay in the middle of the pack and not go off like a racing snake and knacker myself; neither was I going to be at the back of the pack. I was personally quite pleased with my performance. Some of the speed merchants were back in under eight minutes.

During Camp One we were put through our paces in weapons handling, memory retention, map reading, first aid, agility tests, stamina tests, driving ability and a variety of other tests that I could only put down under the classification of sickeners, or what the instructors liked to term 'character building' tests. One of the DS's great ploys was to grind down individuals with personal comments which they then left the students to dwell on. In my room of eight candidates we had one guy with bright ginger hair and another who wore thick black-rimmed glasses. Every time the DS came into the room for whatever reason we had to stand to attention, speak only when spoken to and address the DS as 'Staff'. On every occasion when one of the DS passed the ginger-headed bloke they would look at his hair, make a comment about its colour and another about the fact that it would probably give him away at night – cars would stop by him thinking he was a traffic light, and so on and so forth. The same barrage was thrown at the bloke with the glasses – hints about being noticed for having large specs, comments about being easily pointed out in a crowd, and how in the sunshine the reflection off his glasses would bring instant attraction, and so on. The only abuse I seemed to attract was that I looked and dressed like a 'squaddy', my usual civilian dress being the standard desert boots, jeans and Barbour jacket, the habitual out-of-uniform soldier's uniform. I walked into the room after lunch one day to find these two blokes packing their kit, along with another guy in the corner. I asked them if they were off, and both said they had no chance of passing because the DS had it in for them. The bloke in the corner had decided to go before they even got the chance to start on him! He had been the subject of very little criticism other than the DS looking at him, saying nothing but just make a tutting noise while shaking their heads. It wore him down. I did not encourage them to change their minds. If they were that easily put off, then it was probably best they went. We shook hands, they wished me all the best and off they went. Had they never heard of hair dye or contact lenses? My room was now down to four; one guy had left within an hour on the first day.

Strangely enough, as the days passed, we were allowed more sleep at night, the tests became less exhaustive, and I actually found myself starting to enjoy the process. The instructors' sense of humour began to show through, and at times the scenarios they laid on were hilarious. One such event involved us all having to spend the night out in an observation position, but beforehand there was a twist. We had been told to parade outside the block with swimming trunks and towels at seven o'clock, the con being that we were off for an evening's swimming in the camp pool. I knew something was up as I was aware that the camp did not have a pool. We were then run down to the gymnasium and straight into a boxing ring set-up where we had to 'mill' with an opponent of approximately the same height and weight. 'Milling' involves the two opponents hammering hell out of each other from the time the DS blows a whistle until the second blast, which indicates that the fight should finish. If sufficient effort is not put into the fight the second whistle is delayed until you are really going full throttle, bashing the hell out of each other. My particular fight was with a Royal Marine named Terry, who looked more than capable of looking after himself. I gave as good as I got and our contest was declared a draw. I was quite happy with that; a defeat would have been unacceptable to me.

I was aching like hell and the side of my head was numb from Terry's onslaught. At the end of the milling we were told to report back to the gymnasium in twenty minutes wearing combat jacket, combat trousers, shirt, boots and socks. We were to carry a notebook and pencil, no more, no less.

As we returned to the gym, there were a number of students wearing jumpers and woolly hats, carrying pockets full of Mars bars, flasks, etc. The DS went berserk with those who had pre-empted the night's activities and had disobeyed the instructions they were given. The majority were given a rigid bollocking and had the pleasure of increasing their knowledge of the press-up position for a while. We were told to pair off with the student we had milled with and were then taken to our overnight positions. This was at the back of the camp on the hillside. We were simply shown a plot of bracken and left there, told to make a note of any activity we saw to our front, and that was that. Luckily enough for me, Terry, my Royal Marines sparring partner, was also an Arctic warfare mountain leader, and within fifteen minutes had built us a mini-version of the Dorchester in the bracken. We settled in for a long, freezing-cold night. We chatted and laughed quietly about the milling session. Terry made the comment that one of my punches had dazed him quite badly, and that for a split second during the fight he had suffered double vision. We shook hands and settled in for the night.

About four or five hours later one of the instructors came walking around our positions carrying a tea or soup urn. He poked his head into our little home from home and complimented us on the observation post, then quietly whispered, 'OK, lads, pass out your mugs, I've got some hot soup here,' to which the whispered answer obviously was 'We haven't got any mugs with us, Staff'. The instructor then laughingly whispered back, 'Well, tough fucking shit, then,' and walked off down the hill to pass on the same good news to the next OP position. I must say, even though I would have killed for a mug of soup, I thought the sick prank was hilarious. Just my sense of humour.

About lunch-time the next day a few of the DS had gathered on the road in front of us. As they looked up at our positions one of them let off a 'thunderflash', an explosive stick that simulates a grenade during exercise situations. They shouted at us all to parade on the road. As we started to stroll down the hill the stiffness in my body hit me – I was aching all over, a culmination of Terry's battering and a night out on a freezing-cold mountain with no winter clothing to help fight the conditions. As we paraded next to the four-ton truck the DS told us to get on board. With great difficulty I clambered on to the back and assisted by giving a hand to a few others before sitting down and stretching my legs out straight. It felt great. The driver jumped in the front of the wagon and proceeded to turn over the engine. It failed. The DS then told us to jump off the back and form up at the front of the vehicle – we were to pull it back to camp! Two tug-of-war ropes were hitched to the front of the vehicle and off we went like slaves, another sickener from the DS.

As we pulled the four-tonner in front of the training wing we were told to halt and form up again in teams of four. I wondered what character-building test was coming next; I was not to be disappointed. Stretchers with four jerry-cans filled with water strapped to them were paraded in front of us, and each team was told to pick one up and start doubling away in the direction of the mountainous area. Our team started to walk with its heavy load. The DS went into berserk mode with us, and slowly but surely we built the walk up into a jog. This was not good enough, and the verbal abuse from the instructors continued with a vengeance. We were guided over to a river – 'Get in there, you wankers,' came the instruction, so in we went. 'Now start fucking moving.' Up the freezing cold river our run continued. We slipped, we fell, at one stage we were up to our waists in the water and the stretcher load was becoming unbearable, but we continued. My mind was blank, my body was in total pain. Then, as if some sort of strange cloud had lifted, I was through some kind of threshold, totally free of pain, and found myself thrusting forward. I was totally focused on the run up the river and felt no ache in my body at all – I wanted to go faster! It felt exhilarating, although it was probably downright dangerous. The run came to the end of its course and we were told to drop the stretchers and return to our blocks, shower and change into dry clothes, and after lunch we were to make our way to the education block for a lesson in one of the classrooms.

Returning to my room, after the run I found two more clear bed spaces. They had jacked it in during the night on the OP phase, and had left early in the morning with their one-way travel warrants. A further day and I was in the room by myself. Unfortunately for the last bloke, he had fallen on one of the obstacles going around the assault course for the umpteenth time and had broken his thumb. I now had the complete and undivided attention of the instructors all to myself. Luckily for me, I have a macabre sense of humour and began to react to their sarcasm with a grin at every comment thrown my way.

About ten days into the course the chief instructor had his DS parade us all outside the accommodation block in PT kit again. We were to run another basic fitness test – it appeared to be the last one. I hoped so. There were about eighty people left. As we started the initial part of the run, escorted by the physical training staff, I felt my body ache. My legs were like jelly and the run was a real effort for me. I had put the maximum effort into the physical side of the course and was now feeling it tremendously. As we were let loose for the run back my legs just seemed to be doing their own thing. I kept going. As I approached the end of the run I could hear the PT staff shouting their encouragement to the stragglers, me included. My time was just under fourteen minutes. Bollocks – all that effort just to fail at the last hurdle. We were told to go back to the block and shower, pack our cases and bags and parade back outside in thirty minutes dressed in civilian clothes, leaving our baggage in the hallway. This was done, and along with the other students I stood outside awaiting the arrival of the chief instructor to give us the bad news.

He strolled around the corner and stood in front of us, then quite calmly announced that the numbers he would call out should make their way to the main lecture room; the remainder should stay exactly where they were. I thought to myself, So who passes, those going to the lecture room or those remaining?

He started calling: 102, 104, 109, 111, 119, 123. Shit, that's me! Off I ran and went straight into the designated lecture room. No one spoke, no one even whispered. I sat there waiting to see my mate Ian come bouncing through the door with his inevitable grin; unfortunately he didn't. The chief instructor was then joined by the training major, a nasty bit of work whom the course had nicknamed Damien, the Antichrist. He simply looked at the gathered bunch of worn-out candidates and in his gruff voice stated that we should remain there until the administration staff had had time to clear away the failed students, and then we could return to the block to prepare for the next phase. As an extra bonus for getting this far there would be drinks and sandwiches in the bar at seven o'clock. He then walked towards the door, pausing just prior to leaving the room. Without turning round he announced, 'Gentlemen, if you thought the past few days were a shock, be prepared; there is more, a lot more.' He then continued out of the room. What, no congratulations, no 'well done'?

Seven o'clock arrived and I was half expecting some kind of DS set-up, but true to his word there was beer and there were sandwiches. Some of the DS arrived and had a few beers and a laugh and a joke about the previous few days' activities. I spoke to one of the DS and mentioned that I thought I had completely fudged it by having such a drastic finish time on the last run, when some of the others, who had arrived at the finish point up to five minutes before me, had failed. He made the comment that because I had given a hundred per cent during the course I would not have been expected to have equalled my initial run time; also the fact that someone is extremely fit does not always mean they have the abilities to fulfil the requirements for the job I was to start training for. Whether the thirty-odd people now left were by this stage so mistrustful of what any of the DS either said or suggested I don't know, but within an hour or so the majority of the students had left the bar and had headed back to the accommodation block. Being me, I stayed for a few more beers.

The following morning we were taken to Brize Norton and flown to Aldergrove airport in Northern Ireland. From there we were split into two groups and dispatched to various places in the Province. This was basically an introduction to the Province for those who had never been before. I spent a few days in Bessbrook doing some patrolling in the rural areas, and then a few more days in Londonderry to get the taste of the urban side of the Province. Memories of Strabane and Carrickmore came flooding back. After this phase we returned to the mainland and were transported to a training establishment well hidden from the general public. Camp Two was just about to begin, and would last the next six months.

We were allowed to choose our 'operator names'. With secrecy being one of the major priorities within the unit, every student on the course is allowed to pick a pseudonym to work under. As people announced what they wished to be called one by one, I thought to myself that during the live range periods and the often hair-raising Close-Quarter Battle (CQB) training scenarios I might never react immediately to any name other than my own. In a dangerous situation fluffed split-second decisions could cost lives. I decided to stick with 'Rob', and hoped that no one chose the same name before I had the opportunity to claim it. Luckily for me no one did. We were once again split into three groups. The first group would undertake the basic photography phase, the second were to start the weapons training or CQB phase, and the third would start their progressive driving phase. Each phase lasted ten days and then we were allowed three days off – yippee! On returning after our break the phases rotated until all three were completed. At this stage a few people were back-squadded for a variety of reasons, such as their driving was not to the required standard or their CQB skills were deemed not to have been of an adequate level to allow them to go on to another phase. I was lucky enough to have passed all three phases and continued with the course.

Foot surveillance phases followed, and from there we progressed to mobile surveillance, culminating in exercises combining both skills. This was the nitty-gritty phase. Anyone who was found not to have the required knack was likely to be removed from the course. Training in the art of surveillance took place in both rural and urban areas under the direction of the training staff, all fully accomplished operators themselves. We were given a human target to conduct surveillance on, always one of the instructors. From the first 'take' it was just a case of following as we saw fit, initially. As the phase progressed we would be joined by a member of the DS who would prompt us with suggestions for alternative positions to take up where we could achieve optimum observation of the target, where to walk in relation to their movements, and how generally to conduct ourselves naturally in undertaking what was, after all, an unnatural act. Following someone who calls into shops, enters banks, stops at park benches to read the papers or just sits in a café looking out of a window is a difficult task, particularly when the requirement is to remain completely unseen by the chosen target and at the same time ensure your activities are not observed by any third parties in the immediate area. To do this as a team, within a hostile environment, is an art form. Our foot surveillance drills became more proficient as the weeks passed, with the DS leaving us to develop our individual skills, but still under their ever-watchful eye.

The mobile surveillance lessons were run in a similar fashion to the foot phase, with a member of the DS sat in the rear of the vehicle giving their comments and passing sound advice when it was deemed to be required. This type of surveillance is sometimes more difficult to carry out – the normal course of action to be taken when following a vehicle on a winding country road goes out of the window completely as soon as the task enters the area of a town or city. Along rural roads the priority is to hang back, observing from a comfortable distance, using the natural terrain for cover. In urban areas the team has to close in and make use of other vehicles for cover while ensuring that the target does not have the opportunity to slip away from them because of obstacles such as traffic lights and pelican crossings. Deploying the whole team to drive skilfully and safely along parallel routes while maintaining contact with the target is a necessity. It is one hell of an achievement to get this far in the course, but not everyone reached the required standard. At the mid-course assessment a further ten people left us.

We were left with the nucleus of our group, who would progress to deeper and more detailed phases on all aspects of the skills we had covered previously. I was really beginning to enjoy myself. The course was very good and for the first time in my army career I had found my niche. In fact the emphasis was now more on taking the 'army' out of us. We were, after all, to be deployed as covert surveillance operators in a hostile civilian environment. We had to look and behave as civilians do, but still be able to react to an aggressive situation should one develop. The CQB training reached new levels, the driving skills encompassed methods of escape from hostile scenarios, and the DS became more critical of our dress and appearance. I had been in Bristol on a rainy day on a surveillance exercise wearing my well-worn Barbour jacket. After all, it was raining. On returning to the training establishment one of the instructors asked me why I was wearing it. My reply was obvious; he seemed unimpressed. I also remarked that if I had seen a thousand people today at least two hundred of them had been wearing Barbour jackets. He replied, 'Exactly. You should have been one of the eight hundred that weren't. Be the grey man.' Barbour jackets were seen as the type of clothing off-duty soldiers would wear, so we shouldn't. Barnado's and the Cancer Research shops never had it so good. We all got kitted up there.

One of the funniest situations I encountered during the surveillance phase happened in the middle of a close follow through a major city which had a large ethnic population in the particular patch we were working in. The DS were always watching us and would prompt the students on the radio as to different actions we could take during the follow. Two of the students were doing a superb job of following the designated target and were completely baffling the DS, because however hard they tried they could not pinpoint where the two lads were carrying out their follow from. As the two guys were congratulated on their skills, the DS insisted that they should tell them where they were for the benefit of the rest of the team. They described their location. The DS stated that they were obviously mistaken and that they were not being precise about their present positions. One of the lads came up on the radio and retorted that they were being quite precise and that the two of them were in exactly the position they had reported. With that, the request came over the air that they should make their way to the position where the DS vehicle was parked up. Two characters in kaftans and Afro-style wigs sauntered across the road. It was hilarious. The two blokes had been into a West Indian clothing shop earlier and had bought the outfits. They had purchased the wigs in a joke shop and had put the clothes on in the toilets of a well-known department store, where we had been earlier. Ten out of ten for initiative.

The chief instructor came over to the block one evening for a chat. He mentioned that there were waves of discontent about our unit coming from the hierarchy at Hereford. Because our budget came from the SAS coffers, and because we were an integral part of their group, they had asked that the least we could do was the 'Fan Dance' to prove our mettle. This basically involves 'tabbing' (a forced march) over the Pen-Y-Fan mountain, going down the other side to Talybont reservoir, and then completing the return journey back over the top, all against the clock. Pete, the chief instructor, who was in fact in the Special Air Service himself, had agreed we would do it. However, he would set the rules for us, and his requirement was that we would walk up to the top, have a bite to eat and a brew and walk back down. When we returned that afternoon we could have a barbecue and party at the training establishment. No problem.

The day arrived and we all clambered on to the back of a four-ton truck and headed off to the Storey Arms side of Pen-Y-Fan. For the next few hours we strolled up to its peak. We sat around for a while, had our picnic, and then made the long trek back down to the transport. On arrival at the Storey Arms we jumped back into the truck and headed back to Camp Two, a little knackered but not so worn out that we wouldn't enjoy a few hours' kip followed by a piss-up and a barbecue. We had seen the chefs organising everything on our return. I dumped my kit and lay back on my bed, closed my eyes and drifted off to sleep. One of the DS ran into the block and announced that we had a few hours to go before the party, so we were to be 'crashed out' on a quick surveillance operation in the local area. Fuck me! Kit on, radios on, weapons on, etc. 'The training major wants a quick word with everyone individually before they leave. Rob, can you get over there now.' I rushed around like a lunatic getting my stuff together. I strolled into the main corridor in the administrative block, knocked on the office door and walked in. Both the training major and the chief instructor were in there, and the major briefly told me that he was happy with my progress and envisaged no problems with my passing the course, and asked if I had any brief comments to make. Having nothing to say I was dismissed. On my way out the door Pete told me to go into the orderly room, as there was some mail waiting for me.

Bang! As I walked through the door I found myself being laid into by about half a dozen hooded heavies. I was thrown to the floor, my head was slammed into the ground, and I was pinned down from all angles. I struggled to get free and a thick Geordie accent which belonged to the guy who had his knee in my head told me to 'keep fucking still, you little bastard'. Little? I was six foot and fifteen stone, but I still went down like the proverbial lead balloon. My head had a black hood pulled over it and my wrists and ankles were bound tightly. I was then unceremoniously picked up by the scruff of my neck and my ankles. Whoever had my neck had also grabbed my hair, and I squealed like a pig as I was carried down the corridor and thrown into the boot of a car.

I was driven around for what seemed about an hour, and as the journey progressed I tried to visualise where I was being driven. I concocted an imaginary journey, because in fact I had gone no further than the road around the camp. It's strange what happens to the mind when one or more of your senses are cut off. The boot opened and once again I was roughly lifted out, thrown on some gravel and stripped naked. My clothes were replaced by what felt like rough textured overalls and my wrists and ankles rebound with what I knew to be plasticuffs. I was dragged by my arms along a corridor, my legs trailing behind me and my feet scraping along what felt like a door mat. The people manhandling me were screaming at me to stop dragging my legs, and so I decided that if that was what was making life difficult for them I would keep it up. I slumped my complete dead body weight on them. Fuck them, it was their problem.

I was then shackled to what felt like a wooden duck-board in a room that had a permanent buzz of loudspeakers crackling away so loudly it took away any ability to concentrate – a reconstruction of the white noise used in interrogation situations to stop people thinking between questioning periods. With the gaps in the duck-boards sticking into me it was altogether a fairly uncomfortable and unenjoyable experience. Some time later I was unshackled, lifted up and dragged down the corridor again, dumped in and reshackled to the seat of a plastic hard-backed chair. The hood was lifted. Sat on the other side of the desk in front of me was a rather attractive blonde lady. She started to ask me some questions – who was I, where was I based, who did I work for, what were the names of my comrades, who was my commanding officer, and so on. I decided to ignore all the questions and utter not a single word during this period of interrogation. I was bagged and dragged again, back to the duck-board and my favourite radio station – Radio Interference.

Some time later I was lifted up again and taken to another interrogation room, this time to face a screaming lunatic of a guy who threatened to beat me, torture me and knee-cap me if I did not start talking. My family took a slagging, I took a slagging, my sexual persuasion was questioned – this bloke was really laying it on, and as he shouted in my face particles of spit shot out and showered me. He had a scraggy beard and his breath smelt of cigarette smoke. I would have loved to have head-butted him in the face. His face, however, was always just at a sufficient distance to be out of harm's way – he had obviously been here before. Maybe he had learnt from experience to keep that extra inch away. I hoped so.

This scenario was different to the resistance to interrogation methods the SAS and other élite units undertake, which work on the premise that under the Geneva Convention the only details that must be divulged to your interrogators are 'the big four' – your name, rank, number and date of birth. The briefing we had received some four weeks previously had made the point that because the IRA so far had not signed the Geneva declaration, the best policy under the circumstances was not to get caught at all, and if the worst should happen the maximum amount of violence to free ourselves should be used. The theatre we would be deployed in was outside the bounds of conventional warfare. You could expect to be tortured and in the meantime you hoped like hell that sooner or later the cavalry would come bursting in to take you home to live happily ever after, even if it would be with plastic knee-joints and gas-cooker burn marks on your body. At least you would be alive.

As the hours laboriously dragged by I was subjected to a variety of interrogation methods, ranging from very chatty, friendly questioning through to raving and ranting interrogators. I had given my alibi and cover story. I was reasonably happy with the avenue I had taken, and felt confident and ready for the next bout of yelling and shouting, and sure enough I was soon hoisted off my favourite duck-board yet again. I was aching all over, completely shattered, and was actually glad to have the chance to stretch my legs, even if they were bound together. I felt the plasticuffs being cut away from my wrists and my ankles. The hood was gently lifted over my head. A small sandy-haired bloke with mousey features was sat in front of me. He introduced himself as Wing Commander something or other from the Joint Services Interrogation Wing (JSIW) and proceeded to stare me in the face and announce 'the exercise is over': Yes, my old son, I thought, of course it is. He then said that for the purposes of his documentation he required my real name and details of my real military background. I clammed up. I sat there looking at him as a cup of tea was placed in front of me, and said the square root of fuck all – zero.

He asked me if I understood what he had just said. I stared into space. He then got up walked out into the corridor and brought in one of our DS from the course, and asked if I recognised the gentleman with the white armband and was I aware of the significance of this. I said yes, I did recognise the man. The instructor then left the room. The wing commander sat down again and reiterated his statement about the exercise being finished. For some reason I clammed up again and refused to speak to him. He was beginning to lose his rag with me, and went straight back into the corridor, returning with the chief instructor. Pete looked at me and said, 'Rob, if you don't tell this gentleman what he needs to know, I will. Now be a good boy. We've got the rest of your course to get through and the bar has just opened.' He looked at the winco and said, 'By the way, his real name is Rob Lewis, and he is an armoured corps soldier.' Over the course of about twenty minutes I answered all his questions. I had been under interrogation for just over twenty-four hours and was shagged out. It was Sunday night, and as I walked over to the block I could see a few of my course members in the bar with a couple of the DS. I walked in and joined them. Three from our group had asked to be removed from the course during the interrogation. The remaining gang stayed in the bar until the early hours of Monday morning, and then slept through until Monday evening.

The remaining few weeks were spent on a final exercise and polishing up our recently acquired skills. At completion, when the Director Special Forces walked into the briefing room and congratulated us on passing the selection, I felt, strangely enough, a sense of anticlimax. I had spent the last six to eight months training for and completing selection to an élite covert unit. I would quite happily have started all over again, but there again hindsight is a wonderful thing. Or is it?

I wondered to myself if Toddy would be told of my result by the chief clerk when the signal arrived to inform the regiment I had passed. Unfortunately I never had the chance to tell him to his face – he had left the army while I had been away for the past few months. I returned to my regiment for a long weekend to pick up the rest of my kit, and while I was there met up with Ian – he was not as pissed off as I had thought he was going to be about not passing the course and had settled back into regimental life.

I was quite pleased to drive out of the camp gates – not that I had any grudges, it was just nice to have achieved something that had taken so much effort. I grinned as I watched the guard parade come to attention for the orderly officer to inspect them. I thought to myself, No more of this shit for a while, Robert, me old son.

I was posted to one of the detachments of the Intelligence and Security Group (NI), also known as 14 Int., also known as the Det, also known as the Group.

Chapter 4

The Detachment

I had arrived at the military side of Aldergrove airport late at night with the rest of the successful candidates from my course, fourteen of us in total. Out of our original number of about two hundred who had embarked on the selection process at the pre-camp stage at Sutton Coldfield, twelve of us had made it through to the end. We had a few additional candidates join us at various stages, mostly people who had been back-squadded for a variety of reasons from the previous course. There were also a few others who came on board as well, including two SAS guys, Jake and Terry, who had joined us the day after Camp One had finished. Because of the strenuous selection they undertake for their own particular entrance course, it had been deemed unnecessary for them to go through the buggering-about phase prior to starting the course properly. They had joined us on the day we began the in-depth phases for surveillance, close-quarter battle and driving. They were both extremely competent blokes with whom I got along well. I had shared a room with both of them at the training establishment and had picked up one or two useful points from them, particularly from Jake, who had vast experience within the Province and had been awarded the Military Medal a number of years previously for his part in the killing of some IRA terrorists in the border areas. He had been part of an ambush team that had hidden themselves away in a rural observation post for a number of days, waiting for the volunteers to enter their area and initiate a firing device linked to a vast amount of explosives under a culvert. The bomb was to be used on a passing army or police patrol. On the third day an Active Service Unit (ASU) from the IRA, all heavily armed, were seen making their way to a tree line that overlooked the explosive device. The terrorists were challenged and an exchange of weapons fire took place. The IRA men were killed during the ensuing gun battle.

Terry, an ex-paratrooper, had impressed me during one of the many range periods we were put through at Camp Two. We had a vast amount of ammunition left over at the end of our course and it was decided by Pete, the chief instructor, that we would have a free-for-all range day at Sennybridge and blast the lot away.

All of us at this stage were more than competent with a wide variety of weapons, and the range period was quite good fun. Weapons instructors from normal regiments would have had cardiac arrests at the sight of some of the drills we carried out using live ammunition. We decided to have a run at the electronic range. This was an uphill dash through a gully with a small stream running down it. We were all armed with Heckler and Kochs and our personal weapons, 9mm Browning pistols. The targets would rise quickly as you approached them and would fall when they took a direct hit. Terry went through the range like a dose of salts. Even though the rest of us were very proficient, this bloke was something else, and I remember thinking that if I was in the shit I would want him with me.

I had been allocated with three others blokes from the course to one of the detachments, one that mainly covered the areas of Londonderry and Strabane with a commitment to overlap with the other detachments, so there was coverage Province-wide. The three other trainee operators were Brian, who was an infantry captain, Paul, an infantry senior rank, and Jake, the SAS senior rank. All three were excellent blokes. We arrived at the detachment, which appeared to be a ramshackle set-up, completely innocuous-looking to the outside world. It was entirely self-sufficient within its own confines. It had its own cooks, signallers and mechanics, who provided all the required support to maintain the daily running of the unit without outside assistance – because of the sensitive nature of the everyday tasks undertaken this was a necessity.

As we entered the complex we were met at the gate by one of the support staff, pointed in the direction of the detachment bar, and told that the rest of the operators were awaiting our arrival for a welcome piss-up.

I walked into the bar to be greeted by an old friend of mine from my own regiment. He had been one of the original lads from our COT to attempt selection soon after we had finished in Omagh. He had a huge grin on his face and introduced himself to me by his operator name. The welcome was genuine enough, although during the conversation we had he made it obvious that we should not divulge to the others that we knew each other. I sensed he felt uncomfortable getting into a long conversation with me, even though we had loads to chat about. Slowly but surely all the others in the room made their way to the new arrivals and introduced themselves. I felt quite uneasy. It was almost as if I were being put to the test all over again. I sensed that I was being deeply scrutinised in everything I said and did. It was strange for me to have to act as if I were enjoying their welcome; I wasn't.

After finishing a major piss-up that evening I made my way

to my allocated room at about three in the morning. I swung the door open and was faced with the grim sight of a rickety old army bed with a steel frame, and plain white cotton sheets with the awful brown-and-grey-coloured army-issue blankets on top. My room had a battered old wooden cupboard in one corner and a washbasin in the other. The carpets were threadbare and the whole room had an air of complete emptiness about it, reminding me of the rooms we had in the Apprentice College at Chepstow all those years ago. So this was Special Duties, eh? I lay in bed and thought about the previous six months, and the reaction of the people I had met in the bar that evening. I drifted off into an uneasy sleep. Was it the situation I found myself in, or was it the fact that I was sleeping with the mothball stink of army blankets?

The following day our little gang of four new operators was called into the briefing room and began the process that is termed 'orientation'. This consisted of undertaking a saturation period of information-learning on our area. No time to waste. It was obvious there was to be no settling-in period or slow process to get us on the ground. It was to be done as quickly as possible. The detachment was short of manpower, and we were to be pushed as rapidly as possible into becoming part of the team. I found the amount of information to be absorbed a real problem. Details of the personalities in the area, their vehicles, their addresses, past histories, associates and families, became a blur of facts and figures that just went straight over my head. On top of this we were expected to learn the ground. We had to know all the short cuts as well as the main routes, and identify the addresses and the personalities who lived there on the hoof. As we passed certain areas on drive-pasts, we were expected to rattle off all the information we knew about them – who lived there, what they did, where we were likely to see them and who they would probably be with, what vehicle they were likely to be seen driving, or if they were a passenger who the driver would be. It went on and on.

At the end of every phase we were tested on the information relating to that particular area. I scraped through the first test. As soon as the first area had just about been learnt it was straight on to the next area, then the next, then the next. There was no encouragement, no help. This was each man for himself – get on with it. Debriefs were based on criticism – finger-pointing sessions about what we had done wrong, where we had done it, and what incompetent operators we were for not knowing what we were expected to have accomplished. My head was barely past the first phase – we were now in the fifth or sixth phase and it was not looking good. I battled on with great difficulty and tried to catch up on the information-learning in my spare time, what little there was. One of the first ideas I had had when I had seen the pit of a room I was to live in was to decorate it – buy a new carpet and some second-hand furniture to try to make it a little more homely – and I had decided that without a doubt the first thing to go would be the army blankets. As the clock was ticking away and the pressure was on during orientation I decided to plaster my walls with informa-tion about the area I was to be working in, so that whenever I glanced at any part of the room there would be some kind of reminder – a photograph of a suspected terrorist, a street map of an area I would be working in, details of vehicles and a load more. I had turned into an information freak, but it was still hard going.

Eventually we had the chance to get on the ground as 'one-up' operators. I think the boss only allowed me to join in on the job because he could see I was getting so dejected. The task was to conduct surveillance on an extremely bad-arsed terrorist who lived in the Bogside area of Londonderry, a man who was feared by most people because of his violent lifestyle and unbalanced state of mind. He was expected to visit an accomplice of his and then move on to an unknown destination. I went into the intelligence cell and took one of the briefing sheets on the character to my room and studied it intensely. I learnt off pat exactly where he lived, what car he had, who his close friends and associates were, and his known haunts and activities. I refreshed my memory about everything and anything to do with the area where we were going to start the first part of the surveillance. From there I would just have to go with whatever happened. I felt quite confident. As the team deployed I ran through my head yet again all the relevant points I needed to know. A radio check came over the air and we all answered in turn as we headed into Londonderry. I was passing Ebrington Barracks on the Waterside when I came across my first green army patrol. They had set up a vehicle checkpoint a few yards from the front gate of the camp, and it seemed really strange to approach them. I was dressed in plain, almost scruffy, clothes, had long hair and an array of weaponry in the car which would have brought pleasure to the most ardent gun collector. I joined the queue to pass through the checkpoint. Strangely I was waved through.

I had thought that given my looks and the way I was dressed I was almost certainly a good candidate for being pulled over and questioned. As I drove between the two Land Rovers that formed the checkpoint I thought, If they did not pull me up, then how many other weapons make their way around Londonderry on a daily basis driven by scruffy-looking blokes? A sobering thought.

I passed over the Craigavon Bridge towards the Bogside, turning left along Abercorn Street and following the road towards Rossville Street. Rossville Street had been the place where the Bloody Sunday rioting and shootings had taken place, and my mind drifted back to the day I had seen the kids on television throwing bricks at the troops. It was a very strange feeling to be driving along this dual carriageway, passing the infamous Free Derry wall, a landmark synonymous with all the Troubles over the years. Some of those kids I had watched as a teenager were now likely to be the subject of our surveillance. They were as much dedicated to terrorism as I was against it. The problem was that they were probably better at carrying out terrorism than I was at stopping it, unless I was faced with a one-to-one situation – in that scenario I knew that I could more than hold my own. Another radio check came over the air, and all the call signs *en route* told the operations room where they were and where they were heading. I did likewise. It was a very sobering feeling driving along William Street and heading towards the Creggan – the name itself is enough to conjure up a picture of all the badness associated with Northern Ireland.

After going around the roundabout I parked up facing away from Creggan Heights. My area of responsibility was the route along the direction of the Westway. One of the other, more experienced operators had got straight in and covered the target house – he was termed the 'trigger'. The trigger would be the first to see the target and would give a description of his dress, what vehicle he was using, which direction he would depart in, and any other information he thought it necessary for us to know. We sat for an hour. We sat for two hours. The radio burst into life and a cheerful voice told all the call signs to lift off and return to base. All the call signs replied and, along with the others, I headed back to base.

I had completed my first ever sole surveillance in a hostile environment. Although nothing had happened and we were not required to move after the target I had felt the strain, without really noticing it myself. We returned to our detachment and I nipped into my room to drop off some pieces of equipment.

After that I headed over to the armoury and unloaded the two pistols and the Heckler and Koch machinegun that I had taken on the job with me and handed them in. Next stop was the canteen, where I sorted out a coffee for myself before heading for the debriefing room. As I sat with the rest of the team ready for the debrief I started to pull my jumper off. I was wearing a dark blue T-shirt underneath and as I let the jumper drop to my feet I looked at my shirt. It was soaking wet with sweat – my armpits showed the distinctly deep-crusted white-line circle of caked perspiration, and one of the female operators looked at me and joked about my bodily odour problem. Strangely enough it was a freezing-cold day, but the concentration I had put into the afternoon's activity had made me drip like a tap. At this rate I would never need to visit a sauna again – a quick trip into the Bogside would do the job just as effectively.

The following day the job was to be run again – same target, same team, only this time it would be nearly dusk before we would move into our positions. We all drove by a similar route to the one we had taken the day before, but everyone was to lay up in different locations from where they had been the previous afternoon. I was told by the team leader to cover the route from Creggan towards the Bogside. We waited. Over the radio came the calm voice of the operator who had the trigger position – he informed us of a movement from the target house towards a vehicle of a male who was a 'good possible' for the target. Because it was raining heavily he was not completely sure. Another call sign piped up and offered to drive past and confirm this. As the drive-past was completed confirmation was given that the man who was the subject of our surveillance was indeed in his car and had started moving north-east away from his house. I started my engine and waited for the next location and direction of our subject to come over the radio. As it was transmitted I knew I would never get around to where the team

Sennelager, Germany. Northern Ireland riot training was made as realistic as possible. The shield troops draw the attention of the stone throwing crowd whilst a colleague and I prepare to run forward in an attempt to snatch and arrest a rioter.

Sennelager, Germany. Myself and a colleague take a well earned break during the training. Note at this stage that our padded gloves were not issued, army socks do the trick just as well.

Omagh, Northern Ireland. These two weapons were part of a cache found by members of my troop during a rummage. They were in perfectly good working order and would no doubt have been used in a murderous terrorist attack.

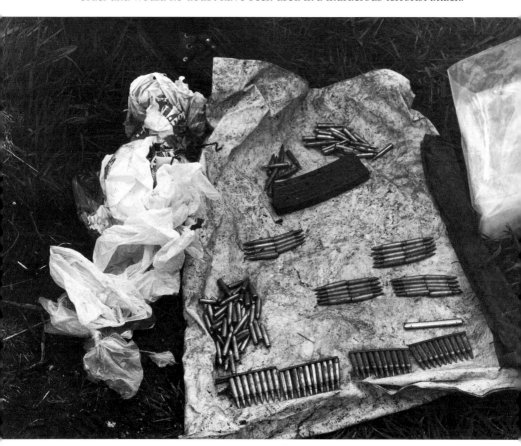

Omagh, Northern Ireland. This assortment of ammunition, clips and the magazine were found alongside the two weapons. They were covered by a plastic fertiliser bag for waterproofing.

(Right) Strabane, Northern Ireland. These two children were playing in a field near to the notorious Head of Town estate. Unfortunately, the likelihood is that they progressed to carrying real weapons.

(Below) Strabane, Northern Ireland. This Landrover had been called out to assist us disperse a small crowd of teenagers who had been throwing bricks at our patrol. As can be seen, the drivers window took a missile before the metal grill was able to be lifted. Note the number of bricks strewn in the road.

Strabane, Northern Ireland. Myself and a colleague chatting inside our base just prior to attending a debrief on the activities of a 24 hour observation we had been on the previous day. The roll carried in my Bergen (backpack) helps to insulate the body from the ground.

Ten hunger strikers who died in the seven month campaign at the Maze prison, Co. Antrim. Their activities dominated the country during my first tour in the Province. Bobby Sands, probably the most noted of the ten, is pictured top right.

Nicosia, Cyprus. This photograph was taken on the runway of the now defunct airport, situated just outside the main city. I completed a six month tour with the United Nations as part of the Scout Car Squadron as a Ferret reconnaissance vehicle commander.

Londonderry, Northern Ireland. The infamous 'Free Derry' wall. The wall, once the end of a row of houses, is located in the middle of a busy dual-carriageway on Rossville Street, scene of 'Bloody Sunday'. Note the army sangar in the background, which is heavily fortified against rocket and grenade attacks.

Ashford, Kent. During one of the CQB scenario training exercises I reversed this vehicle out of an ambush situation whilst another student was trying to get out to fire his weapon. The result was a modified passenger door.

(Above) Ashford, Kent. Myself and a fellow student on the FRU course practising vehicle extraction drills. I am covering him away using a Browning 9mm pistol, the standard personal weapon for all covert operators.

(Left) Ashford, Kent. CQB scenarios are made as realistic as possible. In this photograph myself and a colleague have been surrounded by a crowd after a shooting incident, an attempt is made to get a wounded man into the building whilst I give armed cover.

(Below Left) Ashford, Kent. During the CQB scenario I make a dash to retrieve our vehicle and return to the building to carry out an evacuation of the wounded man.

Enniskillen, Northern Ireland. The Remembrance Day bomb killed eleven people and injured more than sixty others. One of the most cowardly and murderous acts carried out by the IRA in the Province.

Enniskillen, Northern Ireland. The present day scene at the Remembrance Day bombing site since the war memorial has been refurbished and the building where the explosive device was situated completely demolished.

(Above) Fermanagh, Northern Ireland. The detachment when I first arrived, all looking very gung-ho with an assortment of weapons on show including, Heckler & Koch's, general purpose machine guns and pump-action shotguns.

(Left) Continuous personal weapon training with the Browning 9mm pistol throughout the tour was an absolute necessity for ensuring that handling skills were maintained.

Firing the Browning pistol on a regular basis gives the operator faith in his weapon and his shooting abilities, should the requirement to use them ever occur; it also meant you had to clean it regularly.

were heading in time to catch up from behind. I knew I would have a better chance if I headed down at speed towards the Bogside and tagged on from there. I hurtled down the road around a long left-hand bend. There were cars parked up on my left-hand side and it was easier to move over to the right-hand side of the road to make better time. This was a technique we had been taught during the driving phase at the training establishment – at high speed it gives the driver a better view of the road ahead. As I gained speed I became aware of a car coming towards me, and so I gently eased back into the left-hand lane. As I did so another vehicle tried to overtake the oncoming car on the bend coming up the hill. It was on my side of the road heading straight for me. I had to do something quickly. I braked hard. The car skidded on the wet road surface. Smash! I had hit a stationary vehicle on the bend. Shit. I came up on the radio and suffered the major embarrassment of having to announce to the team what had happened. It was one of the worst things I had ever had to do. The team leader asked me if the car was drivable and told me that if it was I should make my way back across to the Waterside. The task was called off so that I could be escorted back to our base by two of the call signs. Londonderry is not the cleverest of places for a covert operator to be stranded with a knackered vehicle full of weaponry. I walked into the operations room to an annoyed audience. The only person with the slightest bit of sympathy was Jake, the SAS bloke. He sat down by me in the briefing room and said not to worry about it – he had wiped out two cars on previous tours and if half the people in the room were honest with themselves they would not have fared any better in the same situation. Tomorrow just had to be a better day.

To compound my problems I was summoned to the boss's office on another matter. He had received a signal from headquarters saying that I was required to appear as a witness at a

District Court Martial back in Germany. While I had been away my regiment had moved to Wolfenbuttel from England. When I was going through my training phase prior to 14 Company selection I had asked to go on a medic's course, thinking it would be useful for my impending selection to special duties. The army, being the well-oiled administrative machine that it is, had got me on a course doing health and safety – not very useful in covert operations. I went anyway. During one of the evenings off, a mate of mine and I had gone up to a little pub just off the north camp area of Aldershot with some of the other course members. Patrick was a fellow rugby player – he was a close friend and had been one of my brother's mates who had stayed in my parents' house before I joined the army. He was also as hard as nails and had a lightning punch.

During the evening three members of the local battalion had made some abusive remark to one of the female members of our course about being with a bunch of 'hats' – the term given to non-airborne trained soldiers. I returned from the gents' toilet just in time to see Patrick knocking one of them out with a right-hander. He had already put one down and the third was being lined up to take a fall as well. As the third bloke took one of Patrick's left hooks his nose crunched and splattered and he joined his friends crumpled up in pain, two of them on the floor and the other holding his face, trying to collect the blood gushing from his nose. Who says paratroopers need their chutes to get dropped? Patrick was arrested by the Royal Military Police later that evening – the three blokes concerned had decided to press charges against him. I was required to attend the court martial as a witness. In all honesty I was really looking forward to it. I needed a rest from the exhausting orientation sessions at the detachment and a chance to get away from the relentless cock-ups I was making. This would be an ideal break, or so I thought. Unfortunately it was to be part of my downfall at the detachment, and did not really help me at all.

The court martial proceedings themselves were quite interesting. It is an extremely formal occasion that requires every person involved to be attired in Service Dress. Mine was rolled up in a box that was somewhere between Germany and Northern Ireland. My old adjutant had to gain special dispensation from the brigade commander for me to attend in civilian clothes and forgo the requirement for a short-back-and-sides haircut. Strangely I was called as a witness for the prosecution, being the only person who had seen most of the fracas from an independent point of view. The barrister whom Patrick had employed to fight his case had 'volunteered' my services to Army Legal Services, stating that he did not require me as his witness. A shrewd move indeed. Patrick was found not guilty of the offences and was promoted soon after returning to regimental duties. I can say with my hand firmly on my heart that I did not lie during the proceedings – I just did not volunteer details of everything I had seen when questioned.

I returned from the court martial to find my three co-students in the detachment all qualified as fully fledged 'one-up' operators. They were out on the ground working alone and had been accepted by the rest. I, on the other hand, was out of date, late and under pressure. I immediately got the feeling on my return that I was very much an outsider. The talk behind my back must have been pretty awesome – to my face it was bad enough. It was not going to work out, and so I thought that before they had the chance to give me the boot I would hand my cards in. I spoke to the boss and explained my position and feelings. He was quite good about it and I probably did him a favour by volunteering to go. Within a few days I was out of the Province, on leave and busily trying to assess my future. I was gutted.

I had been part of the organisation of my dreams for precisely sixty-three days. One of the operators, Bertie, an old hand and third-tour bloke, gave me a sheet of paper and told me to read it some time. It read:

> *It is not the critic who counts, nor the man who points out how the strong man stumbles,*
>> *Or where the doer of deeds could have done better.*
>> *The credit belongs to the man who is actually in the arena, whose face is marred by dust and sweat and blood.*
>> *Who knows great enthusiasm, great devotion and the triumph of achievement.*
>> *And who, at the worst, if he fails at least fails whilst daring greatly,*
>> *so that his place shall never be with those odd and timid souls who know neither victory or defeat.*

I have never been very big on poetry, nor had I ever had romantic delusions of grandeur. These few lines, however, did give me the boost of morale I needed. Thinking of those 'immortal' Hollywood film lines from Arnold Schwarzenegger, I said to myself, Fuck it, I'll be back.

After a few days' leave, I eventually returned to my regimental duties in Wolfenbuttel, Germany. I joined up with my old squadron and tried hard to adjust to the change back to reality. It felt strange to be back in uniform with a short-back-and-sides haircut. I still had itchy feet, though, and knew I would not settle back into life with my old lot so easily or happily. I had seen and done other things, and was not in the mood to go back to 'real soldiering'. There was also a new hierarchy in place, not the same bunch of decent blokes who had been in charge when I left.

One of the warrant officers with whom I had had quite a good rapport going before I left told me to pop into his office for a chat one day. He was now the Intelligence Warrant Officer. He was a fairly laid-back bloke who had a nice enough personality. We were on first-name terms, and when he asked me to nip in and have a chat I thought it was likely to be a fact-finding mission on his part so he would be able to brief potential candidates from the regiment on how they could go about getting on Special Duties. It was, partly. The other reason for his bringing me in was to, as he put it, 'warn me off'. Apparently it had been put around the sergeants' mess that certain senior members wanted me stamped on, in particular the RSM, a thick halfwit, from the Hereford area himself, who had made it quite plain that under no circumstances was I to be promoted and that I would not enter the mess while he was in the chair unless it was as a mess waiter. Fucking great – that was all I needed.

I kept well out of the way. Low profile became the order of the day. It was the only way to get through. My own squadron sergeant-major was an old troop sergeant from the squadron in Hohne, and had been one of the characters involved in the fancy dress party at the retired officer's house in Carrickmore. He had spotted my subdued demeanour. He called me into his office one afternoon for a heart-to-heart chat. After we had discussed the rumours that I had been told about by the Intelligence warrant officer, he said he would find out what was happening and sort it out. In all honesty I told him that I was personally not too bothered. What I did not realise was that he was about to upset the applecart completely.

The following day I was walking past the quartermaster's office towards the NAAFI building when my old troop sergeant from the Omagh days leaned out of his window. Billy had been an extremely good friend for a number of years and had shot from troop sergeant to regimental quartermaster sergeant in meteoric time. He was destined to be the next RSM. I walked into his office expecting a handshake, a chat about the good old days, and a brew. Big shock! He went totally ballistic with me, ranting and raving about how I had mentioned his name to my squadron sergeant-major as one of the so-called crowd who were 'after my arse'. He then had me marching in and out of his office until I reached his standard of being able to halt properly in front of his desk. I think he had just come back from his Guards drill course at Pirbright. When I tried to put my side of the story and explain that his name had not been mentioned, he just told me to shut up and get out. With friends like that, who needs enemies? He used to be a good bloke. It is strange what rank does to some people; sad, really. I think the reality was that because he was destined to be the next RSM he thought he could not be seen to have a corporal as a friend. I was not the only one – apparently he was completely cutting himself off from his old gang and would end up being well hated by just about everyone I knew.

As I left his office I headed back to my accommodation block. As I did so my favourite RSM at the time and the new commanding officer were walking out of my troop's rooms. The RSM collared me and asked who the troop corporal for these rooms was, as if he didn't know. Well, the complaint he had just about knocked me over. Apparently the single lads had dirty washing in their laundry baskets. 'Pardon, sir?' I retorted. 'Yes, Corporal Lewis, you heard me. I have found soiled clothing in the laundry baskets, and I don't want to see it happening again.' The thick bastard then walked off and left the building, and I made my way into my room. I searched through my locker and grabbed my diary, nipped over to the training wing and rang the commanding officer from the training establishment at 14 Company. I explained to him that things back at my regiment were really bad and that if he could get me back to the unit, in any capacity, I would be more than grateful. After a quick conversation he assured me he would try to see what he could do for me, but offered no promises.

Two days later, Screechy the chief clerk sent for me. There had been a signal sent from Headquarters, United Kingdom Land Forces. I was to return to the training establishment. He jokingly asked if I had been making telephone calls to high places, to which I gave the dumb reply 'Whatever could you mean, sir?' He grinned and told me I should start sorting my kit out straight away, as I was due to fly out the following morning. Thank God for that.

I had to collect my travel warrant from him at regimental headquarters early the next morning. Screechy spotted me in the corridor, called me into his office and told me to close the door. He was aware of the hierarchy problems in the regiment at the time. Not just for me; everyone was feeling it, including himself. He just said that for my own good I should make sure I kept away from regimental duties for the next few years. Billy was definitely going to be the next RSM and my life would be pretty shitty when that happened.

The chief clerk was a really sensible guy, one of the few at his level in the regiment at the time who were. I took his words of advice on board and swore to myself that under no circumstances would I return – not until the chaff were out of the way anyway. As if my thoughts needed to be reinforced further, as I walked towards the front door of regimental headquarters I heard my name being called from the RSM's office. 'Lewis, what the fucking hell are you doing in here?' came the pleasant call. I could not resist the chance to tell him I was off, and so turned on my heels and walked, quite smartly, into his office. The sad bastard was polishing a bayonet. He asked me why I was in civvies and where did I think I was going. I told him I was going back to the UK and that I was waiting for my lift. When I explained that I had been recalled to Special Duties his whole attitude changed. He spoke quietly and said that he hoped that I had not taken umbrage for some of the comments he had made. He told me he was only doing his job, then wished me good luck and said that he would hopefully see me in the sergeants' mess one day and we could have a real conversation, and I could tell him about the things I had been up to. I stared at him and told him that I thought that was highly unlikely, but I would be very pleased to meet him at a reunion some time in the future, when we had both left the regiment, and then we really could have a full and frank conversation. I turned and walked out of his office.

The duty driver took me to Hannover and I flew back to England.

Chapter 5

Second Chance

I had arrived back at the training establishment for the detachment just as the new students on the course were starting their first phase on returning from their few days' fact-finding introduction to Northern Ireland. They, like us previously, had spent a few days working in both rural and urban situations. They were about to be split into their three groups for the initial driving, photography and CQB phases. It felt strange to be there again after the period back in Germany, and I asked myself a few searching questions. Was I to be a student from square one? Was I to be part of the DS? Was I just there to be put through a refresher and then possibly deployed back over the water to the Province, but hopefully to a different detachment? I really did not know. I needed some answers to be able to get into the swing of things and down to some serious work.

I made my way straight to the training major's office. He called me in and shook my hand – he had a big smile on his face and he seemed genuinely pleased to see me. Here was a man whose attitude had changed dramatically. Suddenly he was not the Damien character I had once known all those months ago.

That was his alter ego for the course; he was actually a very switched-on and level-headed bloke with a keen sense of humour. We had a long chat about what I had been up to since leaving his training establishment to go to the detachment, and he was particularly interested in what had gone wrong. I think it was useful for him to know why I had not managed to stay at the detachment. After all, he was responsible for training potential operators and it was on his say-so that people were passed and deployed to the operational unit. He seemed, once again, quite genuine in his disappointment that things had not worked out for me quite the way they were meant to, and was surprised that I had not stayed at the detachment. After we had had a long chat, it was decided that if I was going to be redeployed to the Province then I would have to gain the confidence of the students who were on the course at the moment. These would be the people I would be operating alongside in the future, and it was the only way he could see things working. I would start from scratch that day. Fine – if that was the way it had to be, then let's crack on.

I was told to move my kit into one of the four-man rooms and settle in. There was a day to sort out administration for the students returning from the Province and the course, in its three early stages, was to begin the following morning. I moved in to be greeted by the faces of three blokes who had spent the last few weeks being buggered around during the Camp One phase. Their questioning was understandable, but I tried hard to make them see that I was a new student as well. Their knowing looks said everything – they smelt a rat and thought it was yet another ploy by the DS, no matter what I said to convince them otherwise. It was obvious that they were uneasy about this 'new' bloke who had turned up out of the blue. I was not part of the back-squad group and neither was I one of the SAS blokes, so who was I?

Obviously, because I knew what was coming next and tended to pre-empt things to make sure I got in first and did it properly, a lot of my fellow students were under the impression that I was a 'plant'. A few of the DS whom I now knew personally would chat away to me alone about the course content and bring me up to date with things that were going on over the water at the detachments. Obviously, when one of the new students was in the area these private conversations had to be clammed up. This only made the plant story bed itself in further. It was just not going to work. I was yet again in a bit of a dilemma. Then the commanding officer of the training unit called me in one day and we discussed my options. He had been the man whom I had rung from the training wing in Germany. He, like me, was concerned that my retraining was causing some problems. Firstly, because in his opinion I was trying too hard I was bringing unnecessary attention to myself; secondly, in my opinion because some of the students were convinced I was a plant. As far as I was concerned there were no alternatives. I had to keep away from my parent regiment. Failing that, I would leave the army by buying myself out. He looked surprised, and told me that there was probably no need to do anything as drastic as that, not yet anyway.

He had a realistic option to run past me which he thought I might be more than interested in. What he had in mind was that he could arrange for me to attend another course with a completely different unit that carried out its covert operations in the same theatre of Northern Ireland but under its own directive from the Director of Intelligence as opposed to the Director Special Forces. As he described the role of the unit it became apparent that it was the unit that Screechy, the chief clerk back in my own regiment, had told me about, but I could not apply for it directly from there because it was for senior ranks only. I was still a corporal. The commanding officer assured me that he could override this slight problem for me. He told me to take some leave and he would sort out the necessary arrangements and contact me in due course.

I took the time out to wind down, forget the army and selection processes and courses. The only thing I did was to go for the occasional run just to keep my basic fitness ticking over. I had done so much to reach this standard that I was not about to lose it so quickly. I was busy pottering about doing nothing about three weeks later when I received a phone call at home. A rather upper-class voice at the other end asked if he was speaking to Robert Lewis. I replied that he was and asked how I could help him. He introduced himself as Major Brian Thomas from the Specialist Intelligence Wing at the Intelligence Corps Centre in Ashford, and informed me that he had been passed my name and telephone number as someone who would be interested in being invited to attend their selection process. Invited? This sounded good. He confirmed my address and said he would be sending some travel warrants in the post in due course. In the meantime he would arrange for me to attend a one-day interview.

I spent the next few days shifting my mind out of neutral and back into gear. I continued with my physical fitness routine and began to take an interest in the daily news of events in Northern Ireland. The long-expected day arrived and I travelled up to Ashford on the train. I made my way to what is known as 'The Manor'. This old, listed building was the covert home of the Specialist Intelligence Wing (SIW) and housed a number of different departments concerned with everything to do with the sneakier side of military intelligence. I met Major Thomas and had an extremely long and detailed chat with him about my background and personal history, and answered a multitude of questions about my own thoughts on Northern Ireland and the situation there. He closed the interview by telling me that he thought I was a suitable candidate for the next course, but he had to ask me one straightforward question before confirming that I would be acceptable — would I have any qualms or inhibitions about handing money over to people in exchange for information, bearing in mind that some of the people in question might be involved in terrorist activities themselves. I informed him that if the money was being put to good use and if the information that was being paid for was to be used in the fight against a terrorist organisation then I had no moral problems with that at all. All good textbook-answer stuff. He seemed happy with my response and told me that the next course was being run in about three weeks' time. I would receive the joining instructions within the next week or so. With that I left. I had another three weeks off.

The following week a brown-enveloped Ministry of Defence letter arrived at my house in Hereford. I was a little bit put out. It was addressed to 'Corporal' Robert Lewis, followed by my home address. This was, after all, my civilian address. Maybe some clerk thought it was an army married quarter, but considering where I lived and who these people were, I was certainly a little concerned about it. It may seem a bit paranoid to some people, but living in Hereford and receiving Ministry of Defence envelopes declaring your rank really is not a desirable thing to happen.

I arrived back at the Intelligence Corps training centre at Ashford on the Monday evening, and after booking in at the guardroom settled into the Portakabin accommodation. As the night progressed more students arrived for the course, until there were about twelve of us gathered. Everyone made their introductions. There seemed to be about half a dozen Intelligence Corps blokes and the rest, like me, were from a mixture of different regiments and corps. All of them appeared to be a little older than I was and most seemed to be about warrant officer rank. The instructions I had been sent had said that the course was to assemble at nine o'clock the following day. I could not help but think back to the first night at Camp One at the 14 Company selection, and I spent the early part of the evening expecting some hairy-arsed DS to come bursting into the room and throw our kit from our lockers and then demand we did press-ups for half an hour. I had mentioned this briefly to one of the Intelligence Corps warrant officers in our room – he was an old hand at both 14 Company and this unit. He grinned and shook his head, said that I should get my head down and have a good night's sleep – there was going to be nothing like that happening here tonight. The next thing I knew my alarm clock was going off at half past seven and someone at the other end of the room was shouting at me to turn the fucking thing off because they could get another hour's sleep in before getting up.

Our course gathered for coffee in the main briefing room upstairs in The Manor just before nine o'clock. The instructors introduced themselves and shook hands with everyone. I thought, hang on, there has got to be a catch here somewhere. But no – after the opening address from the commanding officer we gradually made our way through general administration, the course photograph was taken, and everyone gave a quick two-minute self-introduction to the rest of the course and the instructors. We then made our way through to the CQB training area where we were tested on all aspects of weapons handling, loading and unloading drills and general safety. Given my previous experience and training, I whipped through this with no problems – it was second nature by now. We were told exactly what the job we would be trained for entailed, and people were given an opportunity at this point to decide if they wished to stay. We were told that if the nature of the employment was not what we were likely to want to be involved in we were at liberty to leave there and then without any recourse. The whole point of the course was to train and deploy covert source- or agent-handlers in the hostile environment of Northern Ireland. Prior to deployment the training would involve instruction in the targeting, recruiting and running of human sources in the Province. The risks of such employment were obvious. No one moved.

As the first day finished we were told of a period to be held that evening which was not on the timetable we had been given. The instructor who announced this alteration to the course smiled with a wry grin as he spoke. Details of this change to plan would be given at seven o'clock in the briefing room. I thought to myself, Yes, it had to be too good to be true and this is it. The fuck-about factor is about to start.

We were each paired off with another student and given a map of the local area. We were then taken by car, driven by one of the instructors, way out into the countryside and given grid references for where we had to get to for the start of the exercise. At the next check-in point we would contact an 'agent', who would give us instructions for the next point, and so on. At the first point we were met by our contact, who instructed us to go to a certain telephone box, at a particular grid reference. We were told that inside the telephone box would be a handwritten note with the location of our next point of contact, and also given a description of a female we were to meet at the location on the note. When we located the female we were to ask her for directions to the next point – she would inform us of the details we required after we had quoted a particular phrase. Off we went to the box. There were no instructions, but standing just to one side of the telephone box, waiting at a bus stop, was a female who fitted exactly the description we had been given by the previous instructor. First lesson in displacement of expectations – never expect things to happen the way you thought they would. Never assume that the obvious will happen.

After an approach had been made it was confirmed that she was our contact, and after a quick chat and briefing from her, we were given our details for the next meeting point to go to. By the time we got there I was knackered. We had been legging it around these country roads in civilian clothes for a few hours, and the jeans I was wearing were chafing the insides of my legs and beginning to bother me quite badly. Eventually, after trogging along for another half-hour, we reached the next point, which was a pub in the middle of nowhere. Our contact was outside with an extremely grim face. He snarled at us that we were fucking late, where the fuck had we been, we could have really put him in danger by making him hang around. This was more like it. He described the next contact to us. He was a Hell's Angel type of character, about six foot four in height with tattoos on both sets of knuckles, and we were to ask him if his wife was still the old slag she had always been. He would then give us our next set of instructions, but only on hearing exactly that phrase. We were told the greaser was in the pub at the bar. Go! Don't hang around. As I walked into the bar I looked around. No Hell's Angel, not even a sniff of a leather jacket, but there were all our instructors in the bar with a well-needed pint of beer and loads of sandwiches for us. All had huge grins on their faces, knowing fully well we had been caught out with the scenario we had been given. This was the second lesson in displacement of expectations. We settled down to a quiet and convivial evening, chatting with the other members of our course and the instructors. It was a great way to start the course properly.

The second day was spent being lectured by an Intelligence Corps sergeant on various aspects of personal security and survival, starting out with very basic examples, such as not putting military clothing out on washing lines at home through to basic anti- and counter-surveillance drills if you thought you were being followed by possibly hostile, unknown third parties. I felt like mentioning the addressing of envelopes but thought better of it. I was certainly in no position to start rocking the boat at this stage – I had too much to lose. The following few days continued in much the same way and turned into a daily session of 'death by view-foil' (theory lessons using an over-head projector). At the end of each afternoon we were taken out for a run by the DS. Once again, with my level of fitness at the time being pretty adequate, this was very much a jog. In the evenings we started basic exercises involving 'chatting up' techniques. Every budding Romeo reading this is probably thinking that this would be a doddle. Believe you me, it is not that straightforward given certain parameters that are laid down prior to the attempt.

We were each individually given the name of a separate military establishment to go to in the general area. The objective of the exercise that evening was to chat up a complete stranger, get details of their home and work locations, get both their home and work telephone numbers, as much detail about their immediate families as possible, and full vehicle information, including the make, type and registration. And then before departing arrange to meet them for another drink later in the week. This had to be accomplished without raising any suspicions or adverse response from our chosen targets. The rules dictated that bar staff were not acceptable targets, and because our course were all men, females were not acceptable either. I was determined to do as well as I possibly could at this task. If the whole point of the unit was to run agents then the ability to gather information on potential sources for recruitment was a real necessity. I knew this exercise would be one of the main tests for the students, and if I could not do this in a friendly area then I had no chance in a hostile environment.

I was given the name of my nominated base. It was a club that was a real dive of a place and the DS were laughing at the choice they had given me prior to my departing. They had told me it was where all the local infantry hung out and was probably the most difficult place for this type of exercise as they would assume I was Military Police. I left the training room and collected my car keys from the clerks' office. I had a quick look at the local map of the area, located the whereabouts of my task and quickly made my way there. I viewed the place from the outside, trying to get a feel of what problems the inside was likely to give me. After a few seconds I thought to myself that there was only one way to find out. I parked the car up just around the corner from the front of the club and walked back down the road. I took a deep breath and walked towards the main door. Somehow knowing I had something like this to do took the enjoyment out of having a pint. I switched on my miniature tape recorder, placed it in my top pocket and strolled into the main bar. Bingo! There was a bloke standing by the bar who had a black bin-liner at his side. As I walked up to the bar I made sure I gave the bag a decent hard kick. I then had the opportunity to apologise for hitting his bag and get talking to him. I was in luck. He was three parts pissed and would not shut up. He told me everything I needed to know within an hour and made a big point of trying to sell me some stolen kit he had. His black bin-liner was full of shirts he had stolen from one of the ferry companies he worked for in Dover. He was a friend of one of the blokes at the base and used the place as his local bar because of the cheap beer. At one stage I had to tell him to hold his conversation while I went to the toilet. My tape needed changing over – he had jabbered away so much I had used one side up and needed to swap it over. The girl who was working behind the bar actually apologised to me for the bloke's persistent rabbiting on about his family and his problems, but for me it was ideal. After a while I knew I had everything needed for the task – there was no point in hanging around and so I made my apologies to my drunken friend and left. I went back to The Manor, wrote up my detailed report using the tape recording I had made, and then handed the completed information in. I was happy with the amount of detail I had gathered on my subject. Later on in the course the instructors ran through the profiles we had prepared from the information we had gathered and I was happy to find out that they were impressed with what I had collated on my target. Some of the other lads had not been so lucky and their reports were pretty scant. I allowed myself a sly grin.

We then spent a lot of time practising the use of covert communications and spot codes, which were used in the day-to-day exercises in the local area. It is far easier to code an area than to use street or place names. For instance, if the subject you are following is walking down the High Street on the left-hand side of the road between Tabernacle Street and the Old Market Street roundabout it can be quite a mouthful to get over on the radio, particularly if other call signs are transmitting information at the same time. It makes more sense to give the locations spot-coded references which everyone is knowledgeable about, so that the same transmission describing the target's route becomes something like 'Blue 21 towards Blue 34 on the left'. Once the area is known well enough and the spot codes are learnt, it becomes second nature. Communications become slicker, and if an emergency arises there is a clearly defined procedure to locate the exact position of any activity.

Tradecraft lessons became more in-depth in their content. In particular, the techniques for targeting a potential source became a subject we were to become particularly well versed in. We spent long hours putting together recruitment plans based on exercise scenarios we were given by the DS, and then spent a number of days carrying out the complete detailed task as a team. Some of these scenarios were based on actual events that had occurred in the operational unit with real sources. Sometimes they worked and the source became part of the scenario, and on other occasions things didn't quite work out as planned and the jobs did not come to a successful ending. This was to be the way of things in the operational unit in the future. It was purely the nature of the beast. The unit's tradecraft involved contact with human sources and not preprogrammed computers. In such scenarios things will, and inevitably do, go wrong.

We were presented with a variety of situations to deal with during meetings with the sources. As well as the operational debrief to gain information about terrorist activities, we were often required to consider the more human side of agent-handling. The personal relationship between the handler and the informant is a very special one – you are ultimately the best friend they are ever likely to have. They cannot talk about their role with anyone other than the handler, and at times the sources become very dependent upon the operative to provide advice on all manner of things, including their domestic affairs. In one of the scenarios I was presented with a female character who was asking me to provide more cash payments in return for her information. Her request was centred around her mother, whom she insisted was in great need of a holiday because of the daily stress and strain of living in a violent area. She suggested that I should give her enough money for a summer cruise. The type of people we would be dealing with in the Province were not likely to just get up and disappear on a cruise when they felt like it. The request had to be tailored to what I knew the woman would be able to explain away should she ever be asked about the excess cash that would enable her to take her mother away. We settled for a week away in a caravan on the coast. Sensible solutions to these types of request were essential to maintaining the relationship, and not drawing undue attention to the source in their own environment was paramount for their own safety.

Because of the risks undertaken in the source-handling we were being trained for, weapons handling had to be first rate. CQB and first-aid scenarios were made as realistic as possible. We practised for hours on all the weapons we would have available to us on deployment, and were trained extensively in unarmed combat skills. All aspects of gunshot wound and trauma situations were taught, rehearsed and practised until they became second nature. If a colleague was down and needed immediate lifesaving treatment, we were all capable of giving it confidently and at the same time dealing with the possibility of an on-going, life-threatening situation.

These situations were sometimes built into exercises. The scene would be set for an emergency source meeting to take place that was, unknown to us, about to go drastically wrong. In one of these scenarios we were told to attend a meeting with a source at a particular place at an exact time, something you would never do in reality. As I drove into the area of the meeting the road was blocked and we were ambushed at an illegal vehicle checkpoint by armed masked men. My natural instinct was to ram the brakes on, reverse at high speed out of the area, throw the car into a one-eighty turn and drive away from the situation at Mach two. My co-handler in the car had different ideas and attempted to get out of the vehicle as I jammed the brakes on and fire his Heckler and Koch machine-pistol at the gunmen. The result was a modernised Volkswagen Golf with the passenger door ripped away and left on a grass bank one hundred metres away from the rest of the vehicle. The door was duly signed by our course and presented to the staff at the training establishment as our leaving present. The last time I saw it it was hanging over the stairs in The Manor, one of the more novel presentations ever made to SIW.

The first-aid scenarios that were laid on occasionally to test our proficiency in this field were quite realistic. We would be involved in a situation when a report would come over the radio informing us of other call signs from our unit who had been involved in some problem that required life-saving first-aid treatment. Once the location had been ascertained the teams would make their way, at all possible speed, to the incident. At any of these scenes it had to be taken into consideration that this was a hostile environment – there was always the risk that more lives might be threatened if the correct drills were not carried out. As well as treating the casualties for a number of different problems, from car crash injuries through to gunshot wounds, we also had to secure their weapons, consider the fact that terrorists might still be in the area, and take any necessary actions to ensure the continued safety of all the operators on the scene, whether they were the injured party or giving treatment.

We then became involved in a long-term scenario in which the group ran through the exercise as an operational detachment, where we practised all the drills and source-handling skills we had learnt during the course, unfortunately including the report-writing and documentation that go with the job. It was an extremely realistic exercise, and by the end of it we were all knackered. The course work continued and was interspersed with recording techniques, anti- and counter-surveillance techniques, more weapons training and CQB.

Then came the mid-course assessment. I was called up to the training major's office. As I walked in he smiled at me and told me to take a seat. He picked up my course notes and the assessments given by the instructors. As he leafed through them he glanced at me and once again smiled. I thought for a moment that this was going to be another case of displacement of expectations and sat back anticipating the worst. He cleared his throat and spoke about my course so far. I was doing well. He envisaged no problems with me completing the course – the only point he felt I should watch was that the instructors thought I had a natural ability to look laid-back and unfussed. This could, in the wrong circumstances, be mistaken for lack of interest. I assured him that this was far from the case and that, even though I might have a relaxed attitude, I was more than interested in the subject and always attentive to the situations in hand. He accepted what I said fully and remarked that all my skills gradings were well above the required standard. Five others from our group departed.

The workload of the course became more and more pressured. Practice source meets went on till the early hours, the sources' information became more complex, report-writing and general reporting became more demanding, and then it was straight into an interrogation scenario. Not for me, though. The ruling is that anyone who has been through the interrogation scenario previously should not have to endure it a second time. The reasons, I was told, were twofold. Firstly, if you have been through the system once you know what's coming and that diminishes the shock impact; secondly, it is generally believed that people start to enjoy the situation and become more at ease with the interrogation process and are tempted to take the interrogators on, knowing that it is an exercise scenario and not a real-life event. There were two others on my course who had also been through this phase at 14 Company, and so with no qualms we three headed into Ashford for a few well-earned beers. The following day, when the other lads had returned from their interrogation period, we had another slack day as they were allowed to rest and catch up on their lost sleep before getting back to the main course.

More weapons handling sessions followed, more in-depth

first-aid training, more detailed and difficult source-handling periods, more long and exhausting reports to write, more rigorous physical training, and finally the end-of-course interview. I had passed.

These interviews were with the chief instructor. He told me that, unusually, the DS were happy to send me to any of the detachments. Most students show a particular aptitude for operations in a specific environment, and the rest of the course had been allocated directly to their detachments. In my case it appeared that they thought I could carry out tasks successfully in both the rural and urban areas. It was my choice.

The chief instructor asked me if I had any preferences as to where I wished to be deployed operationally. I looked at the map of Northern Ireland on his office wall and studied the locations of the detachments intently. I did not at all fancy the idea of going back to Londonderry – the place was jinxed as far as I was concerned. Belfast was a possible option, the only problem being that I never had been one for big cities. I looked at the chief instructor and asked straight away to be deployed to West Detachment in Fermanagh. He said that in the whole time he had been involved in this line of work, nobody – and he stressed again, nobody – had ever volunteered to go to West Detachment. He jokingly questioned my sanity for making this choice, and asked me if there was any particular reason for my decision. I told him I was a keen fisherman. He looked at me carefully and laughed. I looked back at him just as carefully and laughed as well; the thing was, I was deadly serious.

Our course gathered that evening in one of the pubs in the town. The night turned into a major piss-up, and there were some serious hangovers to be dealt with in the morning. I headed for Ashford railway station at about lunch-time that day and picked up a paper to read on my journey home for a few days' leave prior to going back to Northern Ireland. As I scanned the pages I came across a report describing how one police officer had been killed and two others injured in an explosion; both were comfortable. This was a small article on page nine – page nine, for fuck's sake! I seriously questioned the reason for my persistence in wanting to go back to the Province. Was it the kudos, the extra money, the job satisfaction, the chance to save lives, the chance to kill a terrorist, the challenge to be better than my peers? I did not have a conclusive answer then; I still don't now. I suppose it was a little bit of all these factors.

Chapter 6

Fermanagh

After being away from the Province for several months it felt strange to be, once again, in the departure lounge at Heathrow heading back to the 'Emerald Isle'. One of the highlights of flying by civilian aircraft was the added bonus of being able to interchange tickets between British Airways and British Midland at the terminal. British Midland allowed smoking on board and were always more than generous with their drinks allocation. Being partial to both, I always swapped my ticket, even if it meant a longer wait. I flew into Belfast International Airport at Aldergrove at about seven o'clock on a Friday evening. As I made my way down the walkway from the arrivals area to the outside world, I was busily looking around for someone familiar who might have come to pick me up. Prior to my departure from Heathrow I had telephoned the chief clerk at the operational unit and had told him of my impending arrival time. He had said he would arrange for a face I knew to meet me. You really cannot go to airport information and ask them to page the person there to pick up the 'army spy'!

As I walked out into the wet, dismal, grey weather of

Aldergrove, I felt understandably apprehensive. I looked across to the short-term carpark and noticed one of the blokes who had been on my course stood by a dark-coloured Astra. Dave was an Intelligence Corps staff sergeant who had been earmarked to take over as one of the Detachment Sergeant-Majors (DSM) in the future. We had got along quite well. He had been a collator, or spook, as they were known, at one of the detachments at 14 Company prior to going on this selection. We shook hands and jumped in the car. He immediately gave me a rundown on exactly what was in the vehicle. There was a pistol in the glove box with one round 'up the spout', a Heckler and Koch machine-pistol under my seat, also in the 'ready' state, and a full paramedic first-aid pack in the boot. Welcome back! We headed out of the airport area and followed the signs for Lisburn. I was fully under the impression that we were going to head straight down to the Fermanagh area and move into our accommodation. This was to be yet another example of displacement of expectations. Dave told me that Lisburn was the gathering place for anyone in the area on a Friday night to meet up 'on the strip', an area within Thiepval Barracks where a variety of bars were located. The idea was to go 'OTP', or 'on the piss', for the weekend. I really was a bit taken aback by this. Because of my previous upsets at the 14 Company detachment I was not exactly in the mood for dropping myself in the shit on the first day back in the Province with my new unit.

Dave allayed my trepidation by telling me that he had already booked our places in the mess, and my new detachment boss was in the bar and waiting to meet me there anyway, so I would have to turn up. Apparently I was not really expected at work until late on Monday morning, which sounded quite human. I asked him about the mess accommodation and he looked at me and said, 'Well, you are a senior rank now, so you're booked in the mess, Sergeant Lewis.' I recalled Screechy's brief about the one Special Duties job that would accept senior ranks only; here I was. The unit had applied to my own manning and records office for my promotion. They had agreed, and I had been promoted to sergeant that morning with my pay back-dated to the first day of the course, thank you very much.

We ended up walking into what was obviously the middle of a major piss-up in an old Portakabin within Lisburn Garrison which had been decked out quite well as a bar. The majority of the people gathered there were long-haired and scruffy with beards and earrings – and that was just the females! Joking aside, the only thing I really noticed that would have given an outsider the remotest idea that we were within a military set-up was one or two regimental unit plaques behind the bar, one of which was a depiction of the 'Piscatore', with his net and trident. This bar belonged to the 'Fishers of Men'. I had now joined the Force Research Unit (NI).

The unit had been formed in the early part of 1980 as a result of a reorganisation of intelligence agencies within Northern Ireland directed by the then Commander of Land Forces for the Province, General J. M. Glover. General Glover, who was a recognised intelligence expert, saw the need for the military to utilise its own manpower more intensely in the intelligence field, and not to rely solely on information gathered by the police which they then fed into the military system as they deemed necessary. The Force Research Unit (FRU) was his brainchild and became the army's most secret unit, carrying out undercover operations directly aimed at gathering information from human sources or informers. General Glover had written a paper on the trends and likely future development of Provisional terrorist operations. His findings were to form the basis of the antidote to such operations, the Principal feature of which was the ability to gather intelligence directly from within the terrorist organisations themselves. Knowledge is power.

I was introduced to a few of the assembled gang. Most of them were already known to Dave, who had undertaken a number of previous tours in Lisburn. This place was different; there was nothing like the strange reception I had experienced at the 14 Company detachment all that time ago. I instantly felt at ease and knew in myself that things were going to go well. I was introduced to my new boss, Ted, a likeable young captain in the Intelligence Corps who bore a remarkable resemblance to a well-known pop star of the time – the girls loved him. We chatted easily about the course and how I had coped with it, how its content had differed from the 14 detachment selection, and a load of other generalities. We got along well right from the start. He told me, much as Dave had, that there was no particular rush to get down to Fermanagh. There would be plenty of time to see the place over the next few years. I could travel down with Dave or himself either on Saturday or Sunday – it was up to me. I was to relax, have a drink and a good time and get to know the gang.

Saturday afternoon arrived. I was comatose from the previous evening's drinking session. Dave kicked the bottom of my bed, which made my head ache with a vengeance. He gave me some abuse about being a 'tanky wanker' incapable of handling my beer, and told me that brunch was on and to get up and get some food inside me to soak up the beer. It was time to have a shower; he would meet me in the mess for a bite to eat. After the initial hangover had subsided and my body had got the chance to sort itself out with several brews of tea and a cooked breakfast, we decided to head south into the wilds of Fermanagh. We left Lisburn and made our way out to the M1 motorway. About an hour or so later, as we drove into the lakeland area of Enniskillen, my thoughts were immediately focused on a few salient issues. This was the place considered to be the ideal solution to the Troubles, where Catholics and

Protestants tolerated each other and had an understanding of each other's religions and ideals, and where they tried to live together in relative peace. But it had also been the town where, on Remembrance Sunday, 8 November 1987, the Provisional IRA had carried out one of its more cowardly and revolting acts of violence, by setting off a sizeable bomb in the area of the cenotaph, where a large crowd of onlookers had gathered to watch a march-past of men and women from the local UDR, and to hold a service of remembrance for the men and women of the town who had given their lives during the wars. Ironically the people who had made their way to the service that Sunday morning were from both denominations. Eleven innocent civilians were to die and over sixty others were to be injured as a result of that murderous act.

We pulled into the entrance of the military base, situated a few miles to the north of the main town. It was a converted airfield that had been requisitioned by the government many years previously to house troops on a temporary basis; many years later it was still in use. Dave pointed out the Portakabin set-up that was to be my working base for the next few years. He was going to a different detachment not that far away. He dropped me off and we made a tentative arrangement to get together for a beer some time in the near future. I grabbed my suitcase and kit-bag and headed for what appeared to be the main door. It was a ramshackle set-up and the whole area outside was flooded with water. Because the foundations were huge slabs of concrete the rain had nowhere to drain off, and subsequently, even after a few days of fine weather, there were still huge puddles of water lying all over the place. Fermanagh is the ideal holiday location for ducks and subaqua clubs!

The front door had a heavy steel combination lock on the front, and when I knocked a dark-haired little bloke with a northern accent answered. I dodged the puddles, and he looked at me, said he hoped I had brought some wellington boots with me, and then introduced himself as 'Lofty'. He had been expecting me – he knew that I had been at the strip last night and was surprised that I had managed to get to the detachment this early, given his previous experience of Friday nights in the camp. As I walked into the office complex he told me that he was the duty operator and that he would show me around the set-up. It would not take long. Lofty, it transpired, was, like Dave, an Intelligence Corps soldier, and he had been at the detachment for about a year. I wondered if everyone in the set-up was from the 'Green Slime', as the Intelligence Corps had been nicknamed. Luckily there were others at this detachment who were what the Green Slime referred to as 'E2', or non-Intelligence Corps operators. It was, after all, their baby – it belonged to the Director of Military Intelligence, and they liked to have a predominance of their own manpower in the unit. Lofty rang a number from the operations room which was a direct line to the accommodation belonging to our support staff. This was right at the other end of the camp and was a few minutes' walking distance. He asked one of them to come down to the operations room and take over from him for a while. Ryan, one of the collators, arrived and stood in while Lofty issued me with my Browning pistol, magazines and ammunition. Then he said he would take me to my digs.

Considering that I had been used to living in garrisons, barrack rooms, army messes and transit blocks, the set-up here was quite luxurious. Compared to the shit-tip I had had in Londonderry, this was the Dorchester. I had all the comforts of home. The only requirement was that if any detachment operations were to be held here then I would have to clear out of the way for a time; other than that the place was mine.

Lofty looked at me and could obviously tell that I had some reservations about this, although I did not actually say anything. He told me that no one from outside the unit would ever actually be left alone in the place and it was never likely that anything would go missing or be damaged. I should be thankful that for my time with the unit I would have an almost homelike existence for my down time. I was, believe me.

Lofty had arranged a stand-in for Saturday night so that he could show me around the local night spots, an idea I found a bit strange considering the work we were involved in. I had a few reservations, but we headed off into town anyway. Although I had enjoyed limited socialising in Omagh when I was there, it seemed strange to be a British soldier off duty in Northern Ireland. Having arrived in a pub only yards away from the cenotaph in Enniskillen, Lofty proceeded to introduce me to loads of people, with both English accents and Northern Ireland brogues. What the hell was this? After the anonymity of 14 Int., here I was being introduced to all and sundry. They could have been anybody. But my initial fears were quickly dispelled when it became clear who these people were. Quite a few of them were members of my own detachment, both operators and support staff; others were UDR members and some were RUC policemen. Everyone in the place, however, was a Protestant. This was their bar. The social divisions in Northern Ireland, even here in Enniskillen, were still dominant. It was still a case of them and us at a basic level, no matter how the media would like to portray the town and its people.

Monday arrived and I got a lift with Lofty into the detachment. I was told that I would have a few weeks to settle in, get to know the area and learn the intelligence backgrounds of the main areas and characters or players, as anyone either suspected or known to have terrorist links either directly or indirectly was called. I would then be fully briefed by the outgoing handler on every aspect of the intelligence files and the information they contained. After a few weeks of this I would be told which areas and tasks I would become involved in. It was hard work, and a lot of my spare time was taken up in learning every last detail required to complete the orientation. The idea was that when someone was coming to the end of their tour, another person was brought in about six months before they left to ensure continuity.

I had been paired off with another E2 all-arms operator to lead me through my orientation. I was to become his co-handler. Graham was a Geordie, an infantry staff sergeant who was an extremely laid-back character with whom I instantly got on. We were both keen fishermen. His particular hobby was coarse fishing, which is completely different from the branch of the sport that I enjoyed. Nevertheless we had an instant rapport and became ardent drinking partners as well. Graham had an extremely good contact who was able to supply bottles of poteen, the renowned 'white death' alcoholic mix made from potatoes and whatever else comes to hand. This man added fruit flavours to the mix; we agreed that the plum drink was about the best. Grahan had picked up a few bottles to take on leave with him one day, and when I walked in the room at about ten o'clock the night before he was going he asked me, having decided to sample one or two glasses himself, if I fancied a drop. When I got up in the morning Graham was spread over the settee, snoring like a fog horn. On the floor beside him were two empty one-litre bottles that had once held the poteen. We had drunk a litre each yet I was stone-cold sober and had no trace of a hangover. Maybe that was the dangerous bit. I decided to keep well clear of the stuff.

The detachment was quite a small, intimate set-up. Apart from Ted, the boss, there were only four other operators: Lofty, Graham, Ronnie, who was a dour Jock with a similar sense of humor to my own, and me. The other member was the detachment sergeant-major, who was out of theatre on a course in England when I arrived. When he returned to the Province I had quite a shock. This grinning face appeared in the office one day and said, 'Hello, Rob, bet you wouldn't have thought you'd see me again.' Kelvin had been on my 14 Int. selection and had been one of the students to leave at the mid-course point at Camp Two. He was now my detachment warrant officer. He was another of the all-arms candidates from an infantry regiment who had not been able to settle back into his own regiment and, like me, had gone searching for alternative employment within the same field of operations. I looked at him and laughed, and told him that I had thought the unit needed a 'bit of cavalry class', and so here I was.

We had a few Intelligence Corps collators and an Ordnance Corps clerk who dealt with all our administration, along with the detachment mechanic. That was our detachment complete. It was a really good set-up, although to a certain extent we were treated as the poor relations out in the sticks by the other detachments and sometimes by our headquarters staff. The border areas we worked in were a desert for intelligence-gathering, and the communities were tightly knit affairs that were a real nightmare scenario for source-recruiting. The Londonderry and Belfast detachments, on the other hand, reigned supreme. With their permed hairstyles and fast cars, the city detachments were reminiscent of the Bodie and Doyles of yesteryear, dashing about looking cool between hairdresser appointments. We were the tractor-driving country cousins who smelled of cow dung. This situation persisted until the commanding officer, who had personal connections with our area, decided that it was about time we were brought up to the same strength and equipment status as the rest of the unit. Suddenly, over a short period, we were given access to new cars, new radio communications, equipment and weaponry. At last someone at the top had noticed us, but we were still an hour and a half's drive from headquarters. We were out on a limb in one way, but in other respects it was ideal. No one from our headquarters would just pop in on a whim as they did with the other locations – they had to ring ahead and give us prior notice of their intended visits. After all, we could all have been out milking the herd.

I settled into life with my new detachment. I brought a few of the useful experiences I had learnt at 14 Company, as in certain respects our unit was still a little on the rusty side when it came to some aspects of covert operations. Graham and I drove out and map-coded the whole of our area of responsibility, so that at any time we could relate to the operations room exactly where we were without actually divulging the name of a street or a physical point on the ground. I was surprised it had never been done before. Someone joked that because radio communications were so bad in our area you could never tell anyone where you were anyway, and that was not too far from the truth. Everyone learnt the area in the same fashion as we had at Ashford and it worked well – when we could get through on the radio systems. It was the usual excuse with the unit signallers, nicknamed the 'bleeps' – that it was the 'water table' in Fermanagh which limited our communications. We would reply what a load of old bollocks that was – they might just as well blame the 'breakfast table'. They would get really wound up by our abuse, and we would give them a hard time when they visited us and stood around rubbing their chins, trying to come up with solutions. 'Bleep-bating' became a detachment pastime.

The information we extracted from our sources remained classed as fairly low-level, although we had one or two informants who were reporting on the movements and haunts of some well-documented terrorist players. Unfortunately a substantial amount of their reporting concerned established cross-border activities against which we were unable to deploy reactive operations. British Army soldiers were not allowed to cross the border into Southern Ireland.

Our reporting of information was fed into the Province-wide computer system at various security levels. Basically source information is classified by the collators, the informant's identity is completely disguised, and the detachment boss decides at what security level it should be disseminated throughout the various units. If a source of ours had reported that he had been drinking with a well-known terrorist in a particular pub, and at the end of the evening the player had driven home with other known players, we would report this fully to our own HQ at top-security clearance level. At lower levels of dissemination we would perhaps only divulge the registration of the car that the known player was observed driving. At other levels it would be recorded who the player was with and so on. This system was designed to provide security for our source. We would control the release of information in such a way that local intelligence cells would get low-level classified information. Brigade Intelligence would usually get the bigger picture. The Intelligence and Security Group would get further information.

Detachment manpower over the months was to gradually change until by some time in early 1990 I was the only original operator left. The others had finished their tours and had either been posted back to their regiments or had gone to other Intelligence Corps postings, left the army or transferred and gone on to various other courses. A new bunch was in place, and they turned out to be an extremely good crowd. Two of my closest mates were Mike, a Royal Marine with whom I eventually ended up sharing a house, and Ross, a Parachute Regiment guy. We had an instant rapport. We were all extremely professional about our work on the ground and could trust each other implicitly. The main factor in this, I believe, was that we were from an all-arms background and had all been to the Province on normal tours and had not just walked into covert employment; we understood the risks of normal soldiering, whereas in all honesty a lot of the Intelligence Corps blokes did not. They had never spent any time on the ground patrolling as the routine-tour blokes had, and they all acted as if they knew it all. Lofty and I had a serious debate about it one evening. He was a few years younger than me but was close to getting his promotion to staff sergeant, and he thought he had been hard done by not to have been picked up for warrant officer. I told him to 'get real', but he insisted that had he chosen to join a 'teeth-arm' regiment – fighting on the front line – he would still be the same rank. As he said this Ross and Mike walked in and joined in the conversation. Both agreed with me that Lofty was talking out of his arse, and that in his early twenties he could probably expect to be no more than a lance-corporal or a junior corporal. He would not have it. Outside of the Green Slime he knew very little about the big wide world of the British Army!

Ross was to replace Graham as my fishing and drinking partner. This guy could seriously put back the ale – mind you, at the time I was not too shy of the pint glass myself. At a pub one evening he was asked to do some sort of stunt to help raise money for Children in Need. Some of the other blokes were doing one-arm press-ups, sit-ups and a load of other physical shit that did not appeal to Ross. His reply was that he would drink thirty pints of beer before the night was finished. Amazingly, he did. The following evening he went out for a 'quiet' night and drank fifteen pints and then had a few whiskies to finish off.

The boss had noticed our increasingly close bond, which is not a bad thing in a small detachment. Whenever I was team leader on a task, my instant request was that Mike should be my back-up and Ross my cover man. The same happened when it was either of the other two; we stuck together. The boss had observed that it was not going down well with some of the other operators within the detachment. The three musketeers would have to be split up, and he requested that we start bringing other members of the detachment on our jobs. It worked for a while, but eventually we managed to slip back into our little clique. This was, however, soon to be split up for good because of certain events. Mike had been into town one evening and became involved in a punch-up outside a nightclub with some of the local yobbos. He was in the process of taking a severe kicking and had decided to pull his weapon and use it as a deterrent to get himself away. He had withdrawn his Browing pistol from its holster and had pushed it into the face of one of his assailants. The assault stopped. His action, however, sealed his fate with our detachment and he was posted out to another location. In the meantime the boss had decided to split the detachment into various cells. Ross was to become more involved in directly handling a number of the detachment's more useful sources, and I was to become part of the targeting cell, which would mean less time source-handling and more time spent searching intelligence reports for likely agent candidates, putting together recruitment plans and actively 'asking the question' on the ground, face to face with potential sources. It was a risky task. I enjoyed it, but the three amigos were split for good.

I started my targeting cell work and was left alone to go out and actively seek out potential sources. I would do this by reading the source reports generated by our own detachment from the information gathered by our existing accredited agents. I would tour the area we covered and speak to a variety of people I thought might be able to give me suitable leads to follow, usually Military Police corporals who were continuity

NCOs with knowledge of both the outgoing and incoming regiments, the areas they occupied and other intelligence. I would also spend a lot of time in liaison with the intelligence cells which support both the regular army roulement battalions (short-tour battalions) and the UDR. These cells were usually co-located within one unit. From all the information gathered I would put together a targeting plan and submit my ideas to the detachment boss, and then we would go to work. Potential targets for recruitment would normally be people considered to have access to information that was likely to be of use to the intelligence picture, such as close friends and associates of known terrorists, any of the known players rumoured to be disenchanted with the situation in the Province, and neighbours who could report sightings and other low-level information. The ultimate people to recruit as informants were obviously the terrorists themselves. This, however, was not exactly the easiest thing to do, and if a close third party was providing the required information on their activities then this was often considered good enough. It worked well.

Life in the detachment was never routine. Although we did try to arrange meetings with our sources to more or less suit ourselves, the agent was always the main priority. We tried to arrange operations so that their lives were kept as normal as possible. If anyone was going to do the running around, it was us. We spent a great deal of time working evenings, and the odd weekend task was sometimes thrown in for good measure. A normal day, if there ever was such a thing, would consist of arriving at the detachment office at around nine o'clock. If there had been a task on the evening before it was usually late morning before there was any real activity in the office. The boss would be briefed on any worthy information from the previous night and the report-writing would begin. We would spend a great deal of time looking for new routes and safe meeting places for the agents; as they say, time spent on a recce is seldom wasted. After a few years I knew the area better than most locals.

As well as the report-writing on source information from the last task, operational planning for the next job had to be carried out, and there was always an array of administrative chores to be undertaken. Weapons had to be kept in full working condition and weekly range periods were organised to test-fire all the firearms we used. Covert communications had to be tested prior to departing the detachment on operations, and vehicles had to be kept in serviceable order. All work and no play, as the old saying goes.

My particular play was fishing. I would relish every free moment walking along a riverbank, casting a fly precariously on the nose of a wild brown trout and feeling the tug of the line as the fish began its battle. After days of working in an environment of violence, terrorists, weapons and informants, it was the best possible way to unwind and relax. Unfortunately, trouble was always a possibility, and so my personal weapon always came with me. Even when I was loch-fishing miles away from any urban areas the Browning pistol was at my right hip, hidden away in its holster. It became part of my life, and it was always a strange feeling when I was away without it. Taking leave away from the Province was always a problem, as once again the priority was the source. It was not permissible for a handler and co-handler to be away at the same time in case their particular agent requested a meeting, which often meant long periods of time without being able to get away from work.

The unit was always good for the occasional social night. When a handler was due to leave the Province invites to parties at the various detachments were sent out. They were always raucous affairs, which invariably went on through the night and sometimes finished the following afternoon. The adage of work hard, play hard was seldom ignored.

Chapter 7

'BRITISH SPIES STALK BORDER'

'BRITISH SPIES STALK BORDER' read the major headline in one of the many republican newspapers in Northern Ireland the week following one of the source recruitment operations our detachment had carried out. A few other similar papers, including the infamous *An Phoblacht* (*Republican News*), claimed comparable stories, with headlines like 'GIRL HITCHHIKER OFFERED BRIBE BY BRITISH IN-TELLIGENCE' and 'BRIT AGENTS TRIED TO BRIBE GIRL TO SPY'. It appeared we had caused a local outburst of nationalist outrage. The story was that British Intelligence agents had tried to offer a bribe of money in exchange for information to a young female hitchhiker who lived in the area to the south-west. The bare facts of the articles were in fact quite correct. We had attempted to gain another source of informa-tion on the movements and lifestyles of certain individuals involved in terrorist activities in the area where she lived, and in particular someone whom we knew she was personally in-volved with. This, of course, was the whole reason for our being there. We, as a covert unit, actively targeted individuals whom we believed had the potential to be informants on a regular basis, finding out who they were, where they worked, who the members of their family were, what they knew, and primarily what connections they had with any of the terrorist organisations.

With this information painstakingly put together over a period of weeks, sometimes months, firstly by the collators and then updated on a daily basis by the recruitment team, the potential human targets we had selected for recruitment were short-listed. Then, eventually, when sufficient background work had been completed, a formal request was sent up to the 'head shed' at Headquarters Northern Ireland in Lisburn.

Authority for a recruitment attempt would then be awaited. These requests would be presented to a committee made up of both military and police personnel. The Special Branch officers covering our area were also consulted about the attempts that we were likely to be making. We were controlled by British Army Intelligence, which would ultimately make the decision for us, but Special Branch were generally kept aware of who our informants and potential targets were. In fact they were aware of most of our intelligence through their own resources. I had very little time for them, even though we tried to establish a rapport with them on many occasions and fulfil our obligations. My personal opinion was that the Special Branch did not always play ball with us as much as they could have done. If they had, it is just possible that greater inroads might have been made during my tour.

The reason for our having to gain permission to recruit through the committee system was that other agencies of a higher authority might also have an interest in the same person, and would on the majority of occasions be given priority over us, even though we were supposedly supporting each other in the fight against terrorism. This restriction on some of our operations was sometimes really annoying; for me it reinforced the thinking behind General Glover's speculation that an independent covert military force might be more competent at carrying out such intelligence tasks without interference from outside influences. As someone once quipped, 'A camel was a horse designed by a committee.' How right they were.

Information that a female known to be living in the southwestern area of our patch was the close friend of a man who was confirmed to be a fully fledged Provisional terrorist had been passed on to us by one of our existing informants. The girl lived in a little village that housed a close-knit nationalist community, one of the places where the green troops on foot patrol knew they would incur problems of one sort or another. It was a known hive of republican activity, and was situated a short distance from one of the authorised border crossing points. The name of the terrorist was well known at the time to the security forces; he was one of the IRA's most noted players. He was on a list of terrorists to be arrested on sight, an unlikely eventuality given that someone of his background was very thorough and professional when it came to carrying out his day-to-day activities without risk of capture.

In the South the terrorists' protection is guaranteed by their own kind. Their existence is maintained by moving between safe houses and temporary accommodation provided by their fraternity and by their own families and friends. The terrorist community in the Province has over many years built up an intelligence network second to none, keeping track of both police and military movements in the border areas, making the chances of this man actually being foolish enough to cross into the North very remote. Even if he did, it was highly likely that he would enter through one of the many illegal border crossing points, or possibly gain entry without the uniformed troops being aware of who he was. He was a dedicated professional terrorist, after all, and if he were to cross into the Province it would be for one reason only. To carry out an attack of some kind on a military or police establishment, or (and this was more often the case) a soft target – an off-duty member of the security forces.

The fact that he had a young female friend travelling into our patch on a daily basis was now of great interest to our detachment, and so we set about the task of gathering as much information on her as possible with great enthusiasm. We found out every little detail about her to give us the opportunity of recruiting someone who might be able to give us a decent break into an IRA ASU, gain inside information on their movements, habits, planning procedures, associates and, more to the point, any operations they would be carrying out – the point being to intercept these acts of terrorism and turn the situation to our own advantage. Life, unfortunately, is not that simple, especially when it concerns an organisation that keeps its secrets well, has a policy of limited dissemination of information on its operations, and is not known to treat informants with any degree of forgiveness if they are discovered. The IRA has rules laid down in what is termed the 'Green Book', which is effectively a set of guidelines and instructions on which they base their lifestyle within their organisation. They take it very seriously. Basically it is the equivalent of a military-style list of commandments, a 'hearts and minds' directive that covers all the requirements demanded of the Provisional IRA volunteers in much the same way as the Queen's Regulations makes similar demands on men and women serving in the British armed forces. These include orders on how a member should live his life, what he should do if he is arrested, when members can carry out operations and even how to conduct themselves at funerals. The rules are binding, and breach of them carries penalties ranging from dismissal from the organisation through to death. This man would live by those rules implicitly and would be a hard person to track down and monitor. Here was the chance.

The source of the information we had received about the girl, a man named Michael who had been working for our organisation for many years, was now met on a more frequent basis. He was usually debriefed on his activities fortnightly; this was stepped up to once or sometimes twice a week. He was aware of our great interest in the girl and understood the reasons for us needing more frequent meetings. He had in the past often come up with useful pieces of intelligence which had been used to good effect within the Province. From him we knew where she worked, how she travelled, where she went drinking in the evenings, and a host of other useful details concerning her close family and friends. The big break was that here was a female who had direct access to a Provisional IRA terrorist. We were more than determined to recruit her into our organisation. The problem was how?

Over the next few weeks one of our collators was deployed on a regular basis to the area that we knew the girl would travel through and began to set about the initial task of 'befriending' her. The primary objective of this was to get the information that Michael had passed to us corroborated, to ascertain her daily movements, and generally to get a first-hand feel for her attitudes and general character. Did she like her job? How much was she paid? Did she have a bank or building society account? Did she have a boyfriend? What were her feelings on the Troubles? The list is endless, but it gives a necessary background picture of the character we would be trying to deal with.

The collators performed an essential and integral part of our covert operations. They basically did the donkey work and then briefed us, the operators, on the information they had gathered and their views on the way forward. They would travel down to the patrol area and spend a few hours each day in uniform carrying out their task. Their skills at talent-spotting tasks were fundamental to our missions, and they were usually more aware of the 'big picture' than anyone else within the detachment. They would, however, be left out of the actual recruitment operation. This would be carried out by our specialised team, which had the training and experience to tackle what, at the end of the day, was an extremely dangerous business. A large number of collators who spend time with the detachments of both 14 Company and the FRU invariably have a go at the selection process themselves, and the majority have turned out to be very effective operators.

During one of our regular Friday afternoon 'prayer' sessions the decision to go ahead with the attempt to recruit this girl was taken. 'Prayers' was the term given to the weekly meetings where everyone was involved in the updating of events concerning all aspects of detachment life, both operationally and administratively, and sometimes socially. Everyone had the opportunity to put forward ideas and comments, from the boss and the DSM down through the operators, the collators, the clerks and the mechanics. This involvement ended when the serious operational discussions were about to take place. At this stage the administrative staff were thanked for gracing us with their presence and were asked politely to leave so that the nitty-gritty of the operation we were involved in could be discussed behind closed doors.

During this particular prayer session in June 1990 the phone rang in the operations room. The collator who was manning the desk at the time interrupted our meeting to tell the boss that the operations officer was on the line and wished to speak to him. A few jokes were exchanged about the boss obviously being up for promotion which had come through, or alternatively facing the sack for being seen with an offensive female at a dinner party in the officers' mess. He returned to the prayer session after about ten minutes, having spoken to the unit commanding officer and the operations officer in Lisburn. They had cleared the recruitment operation.

Because of the breakdown of the detachment into various operational cells, the task of the girl's recruitment was handed entirely to me. The boss basically gave me a free hand in the planning, preparation and eventual execution of the operation. I planned everything down to the last detail. The initial recruitment of a potential informant is usually a safe enough task. You have the element of surprise on your side, your background work is done, and you are usually in total control of the situation. The target would not be aware that any such approach is likely to happen. The really risky business is the first meeting you hold after that initial approach. It is fraught with dangers. If they have agreed to meet you after the recruitment approach there are serious questions that have to be asked. Is it a set-up, either at the wrong end of a journalist's camera or a terrorist's Armalite rifle? The possibility is always there. After all, these are people with real terrorist connections – the killing of a source recruiter or handler would bring a great deal of kudos to their ranks.

The first phase of the operation was to carry out physical surveillance on the target. We were aware that the girl caught a bus going through a particularly notorious area every weekday morning at about nine o'clock. She would invariably jump off the bus, which then continued along its route. She would continue walking along the main road towards where we would be waiting and would start hitchhiking, invariably being picked up by someone driving in the same direction. She would travel with whoever gave her a lift until they reached the built-up area of the town about fifteen minutes later, when she would usually be dropped off near a bridge by the lights that controlled the heavy traffic flow into the shopping area of town. From here it was a short walk over the bridge and into the main street. She would get into work at about twenty past nine.

The girl would always be sighted again at lunch-time, usually walking to a café in the busy shopping centre, an area in the middle of the town, or sometimes entering a pub in the same area known for its nationalist patronage. Her lunch break would last an hour or so, then she would walk back to work and would not be seen again until just before half past five, when she would be observed leaving work, making her way back over the bridge and heading out on the main road. Sometimes she would jump on the bus, and on other occasions would thumb a lift from anyone heading in the same direction.

This pattern of life was noted by our surveillance team over a period of a few weeks and formed the starting point for the recruitment attempt. It was decided that we would carry out the task in a completely covert manner. In the past some sources had been successfully 'chatted up' in public places. The café and the pub where she spent her lunch breaks, however, were both considered to be too close to her workplace – she probably would not feel comfortable with this kind of approach. It was decided that the initial approach should be made either as she was walking after getting off the bus in the morning or on the return journey as she walked from work in the evening. After all the various options had been considered and discussed with the boss, I was left with the unenviable job of starting to write up the in-depth orders for the recruitment task. This would include everything the team involved would be expected to do – what specialist equipment was required, how the task would be carried out, and the timings we would be working to. I tried to consider all the possible eventualities. Should any occur, at least we would hopefully all know how to react to the situation.

I had requested the use of a female partner for the job, and a girl from one of the city detachments, Katie, had been seconded to us for the duration of the whole operation. She had been in the job for a number of years, and I knew that she was more than competent. After all, the girls in the unit had been through all the same training as we blokes had, and they were ideal for cover on these occasions.

The operation orders took me about two full days to put together, and then I had to get the team organised to do their ground recces and dry runs. We spent several hours going through the various scenarios that we were likely to deal with.

What if she screams rape?

What if she tries to run off?

What if she attacks me or Katie?

What if she does not turn up that day?

What if she refuses to speak?

And then the real cruncher – what if she says yes?!

The decision was made that the attempt would be carried out as she left the bus and made her way by foot towards her workplace. We would try to intercept her between the bus drop-off and her walk, getting in before someone else picked her up as she started to hitchhike. There was about a fifteen-minute drive into the main part of the town, and we needed to make sure she got to work on time so as not to raise any undue suspicion should the attempt be a success. Therefore I had to convince her during the fifteen-minute journey and make an arrangement for a follow-up meeting as soon as humanly possible. This was not going to be easy. On the Tuesday morning we held a 'dry run' with the boss acting as the girl. He vetoed my idea that he should wear a skirt and shave his legs for realism. We went through the entire operation adhering to virtually the exact timescale we would be operating to the following day, when it would be for real. It gave us a useful indication of other traffic likely to be in the area, who else would be on foot walking around, and who, if anybody, would take notice of our team or the girl. The only tactical difference for the dry run was that we used different vehicles from those to be deployed on the actual job. Everything else was an exact mirror image. It was a very useful exercise and I felt quietly confident about how it had gone. After the practice run we gathered at the detachment for a full hands-on debrief. The operators who were involved were constructive in their limited questioning of one or two minor points that needed ironing out, and I only needed to make slight changes to my detailed orders in a few places. Thank God.

That evening the whole detachment was gathered in the operations room for my briefing. Just about everyone was involved for a variety of reasons. In the operations room itself the detachment warrant officer would be running the desk. Steve was an old sweat at the organisation and had vast previous experience of such recruitments. He had been awarded a Gallantry Medal some years previously for various escapades he had been involved in within the Province. He was to be the link man for the whole team, keeping everyone involved informed over the radio as to what was going on out on the ground. He was also responsible for organising the deployment of our back-up teams should something go wrong and the shit hit the fan. In the operations room with him he had one of the collators — Terry would be writing up the radio log and recording the whole job as it progressed. He was also in direct contact with the headquarters staff should anyone at the head shed feel the need to find out what was going on. Thankfully they usually kept their noses out of operations until after the event. He would also be useful for some other major priorities, like making Steve's coffee and fetching his cigarettes! The detachment mechanic was on stand-by with his recovery van, should he be required. If this were the case, then one of the operators not involved directly in the task would go out on the ground with him as his passenger. This would enable the mechanic to carry out his work with a trained operator carrying various types of weaponry to act as his close cover. The operator would be someone who knew the area well and who would be aware of the exact location that the recruitment task had proceeded to. The 'on task' team consisted of myself and Katie in the pick-up vehicle, Ross in the front cover car and Lofty in the drop-off point cover car. The rest of the team consisted of Ted, the boss along with Alan in the rear cover car, and two of the collators in uniform on the road as part of a patrol set-up. On completion of the detailed orders everyone was given the opportunity to ask questions, offer advice and throw in any suggestions they might have.

The operation would require the two collators to leave earlier than the rest of the team and make their way to the area we would be working in, where they would assume the role of the search-and-chat soldiers on the road. The patrol was laid out in such a manner that vehicles in the queue wishing to proceed towards the town could not see the vehicles ahead of them. Therefore the covert vehicle being driven by our two collators could be reversed into the compound where the troops live out of sight from anyone on the road. The two lads would then give the military commander on the ground a quick brief and tell him their requirements. They were then to get into uniform and assume command of the location.

At this point the area would be cleared of the soldiers from the resident battalion, who would be confined to their living quarters and cookhouse for the duration of the task. Soldiers by nature are a nosey bunch, and always more so if they think something sneaky is going on. Our two collators were in touch by radio with all of our team and knew exactly when we were due to arrive.

The main team left the detachment in four vehicles, with the drop-off point cover car remaining in position along the way. We all took different routes to the designated area and arrived separately, with the boss and Alan arriving at the locality first and reversing their car to enable them to become the rear cover car on deployment. Katie and I arrived in our vehicle. This was a blue Ford Orion, which was the operational car belonging to one of the lads who was soon to be leaving the Province. Because of the nature of this particular job the vehicle was undoubtedly going to be compromised, and it would not be too much of a problem for this car to be lost. For a little bit of extra cover our mechanic made up a set of false number plates. This was later to be mentioned in several local papers, and the Sinn Fein councillor, Paul Corrigan, made quite a big fuss about the whole thing. Funnily enough so did Special Branch. We thought it was highly amusing.

The final team car into the area was driven by Ross, a well-trusted mate of mine. I had asked for him to be the front cover car. His task would be to go ahead of us, to make sure that any police, army or UDR road checks were located, informed immediately of the operation in progress and asked to get off the road and out of the way. In the past we had instigated complete out-of-bounds areas in places where we were working, only to find that patrols from a variety of agencies would enter the area to see what was going on, an extremely stupid and dangerous activity considering the sensitive nature of the tasks we were often carrying out. So with this in mind it was decided not to put the area of the operation out of bounds as it would surely draw attention to our task and possibly the identity of the target.

After getting the whole operational team into place, it then became a waiting game. We hung about for about an hour or so in the cover of our locations, drinking coffee, smoking and chatting, until one of the collators strolled into the area where we were parked up and informed me that the girl had just been seen getting off the bus and was walking her normal route. Time to go!

As she walked through the area, our collator had his normal quick conversation with her. He asked some pretty general questions and then without too much delay allowed her to proceed. All the traffic heading from that area towards us was then halted. Any vehicles waiting to travel in the other direction were let through speedily in order to clear the road. I asked the team to give her a few minutes to get along the road, and eventually told Ross to make his move. He drove out through our area, poked his tongue out and gave a one-fingered salute as he passed us, and headed towards where the girl was walking. After about two minutes he passed a message on the radio to the effect that she was a few hundred metres up the road on the left and was obviously looking for a lift. She appeared to be a bit upset that he had not stopped and picked her up on his way past. The road was completely barren of vehicles and people. Stand by!

Katie and I left the compound, with her driving and me in the front passenger seat. As we approached the girl she turned; her thumb went out and she stared directly at us. Katie pulled the car over and I leaned back to open the rear passenger door. Katie asked her if she was heading into town, to which she replied yes and confirmed that she would like a lift. Once she was in the rear of the car I turned around and proceeded to tell her some of the details we knew about her. I introduced myself as someone who worked for an intelligence organisation. She looked extremely shocked, to say the least. I went on that we knew of some pretty nasty characters to whom she was close, and that if she was able to give us some information on these people and their movements there could be some reward for providing such detail. She told me that she was not the girl I had mentioned by name, and wanted to know who these people I wanted information on were. She denied knowing anyone who was likely to be of interest to us, whoever we were. As the journey progressed, and with a little prodding from Katie, she did finally admit who she was, and agreed to meet us again, but not that evening. This all seemed to be going reasonably to plan. I was aware of the cover vehicles in front and behind us doing their bit. Time passes extremely quickly when you are under pressure in this kind of job, and so it was not long after we started our approach into the built-up urban area that I decided that the time was right to hand over a cigarette packet containing two hundred pounds and a message to ring me on a telephone number I had written on the side. This number related to a new line at the detachment used solely for source-recruiting operations. At the drop-off point on the bridge Lofty, in the cover car, assumed control, putting the girl under surveillance, with the rear cover car joining in to ascertain where she went after being dropped off by us. Ross, in the front car, peeled off left in the opposite direction, and we continued over the bridge, following the road passing the RUC station, and returned to the detachment. The other members of the team arrived back about twenty minutes after us to say that the girl had literally legged it up the road and had run straight into work.

We all congregated in the operations room for the debrief. Had we got a result? Was she going to meet us? We played the tape of the conversation in the car and discussed the options for the next phase. We decided that to try to pick her up on the way home that evening might be a little too unnerving for her, and so it was agreed that I would make an approach as she left her workplace and made her way to the main road the following evening. This, however, is possibly the most dangerous phase of any such recruitment operation. She was aware of my identity and would recognise me straight away. She was also aware that it was highly likely that another approach would be made sooner rather than later.

That same evening, after everyone else had cleared off

down the pub, I rewrote the detailed orders for the following day. This time they were to include the possibility of a set-up aimed at me directly. We had to account for all the worst eventualities, whether a public relations trap set by the republican movement or, the worst scenario of all, a reactive situation carried out by terrorists. Extra manpower was enrolled from some of the other detachments and another covert vehicle borrowed from our headquarters in Lisburn to contain our own reactive team, should things get really out of hand. We also had the assistance of a Gazelle helicopter fitted with an immensely powerful optical sight, from which one of our operators would be able to see and control the movements of both me and the girl, along with the rest of the team. Also, in the event of a reactive situation, the helicopter would function as highly effective medical evacuation transport. We spoke to the commanding officer of the local regular battalion, and he was more than happy to let us have the use of his battalion's QRF, which, under the direction of one of our operators acting as liaison officer, could be deployed to cut off any terrorists who were lucky enough to make it away from the scene should a reactive attempt of this kind be made. They were located in the local barracks, within a few yards of a Wessex helicopter sitting ready and waiting to go on the liaison officer's word.

I eventually managed to finish the orders by about four in the morning. I had decided to get my head down when the first of the helicopters started to arrive at the camp to begin their day's work. Lynx and Wessex helicopters flying in across the top of the Portakabin operations room did not exactly make for conducive conditions for a good few hours' sleep. However, I was completely shagged out, and the next thing I knew was Ryan, one of the collators, asking me how many sugars I wanted in my coffee. I think you could have marched the massed bands of the Brigade of Guards past me during those few hours and I still would have slept through it.

And so the next phase was ready, only this time the briefings I had to give encompassed greater detail, and of course there was extra manpower to be brought into the picture. The brief for the QRF was left to the liaison officer and was fairly limited in its content — all they were really aware of was that if the job somehow went wrong they would be deployed to kill terrorists, a highly entertaining thought for soldiers. I'm sure it made their day. I, however, was more concerned that our operational team were being deployed in every possible nook and cranny to watch my arse. They were all competent blokes, and they knew exactly what was going on. This type of operation always has its attractions for the desk pilots at headquarters, and once the boss had spoken to them to inform them of the on-going scenario they decided to be there, of course. The operations officer and the assistant operations officer arrived early the following day, as is their prerogative, and proceeded to question me inside out about this, that and the other. I really felt like telling them to piss off and to wait for the report to get to them at the end of the job. But I answered their questions firmly and professionally, and made them welcome as part of the operational team.

On the evening of the operation all the call signs involved were deployed to the area of the second recruitment approach. The Gazelle helicopter was hovering a few thousand feet above us, and the soldiers who made up the QRF were busily trying to interrogate our liaison officer about how many terrorists they were likely to encounter. I was parked up around the corner out of sight from the area of the bridge, but in direct sight of our close cover team and two other covert vehicles. Over the earpiece in my left ear I heard the call 'Stand by, stand by'. This was the signal to inform me that the girl was leaving work, and so with a quick nod to my close cover I proceeded on foot from the carpark towards the bridge. I caught sight of another of my cover men leaning over the bridge, chatting to one of the girls borrowed from another detachment. They were armed with Heckler and Koch MP5K machine-pistols. These weapons are very compact in size and are easily hidden beneath a bulky jacket. When suspended over the shoulder under the jacket, held by an elastic bungee hooked to the rear swivels, they can be brought directly into use with great ease. Both were watching my route all the way and informing me on the radio that they could see nothing untoward.

My earpiece burst into life again as the talk-through of the girl's movements was continually transmitted:

'All calls, Echo One [the girl] is foxtrot on the left towards blue one-nine.'

'Zero, roger that.'

'That's Echo One still foxtrot, blue jeans, long dark coat carrying a blue shoulder bag.'

'Zero, roger.'

'Echo One approaching blue one-nine.'

'Echo One at blue one-nine towards blue four-two.'

'Zero, that's Echo One towards blue four-two. Romeo acknowledge.'

'Romeo, roger,' I answered, to confirm I knew the girl's exact location.

At times like this, when the target is moving into the area where the recruiter is easy prey should a terrorist attack be carried out, it is a pretty hairy situation. My heart was pumping and the adrenalin flowing. It is also a time when a sense of humour within the team is appreciated. The next radio call came from the cover team on the bridge:

'All calls, this is Kilo. Echo One is wearing heavy lipstick and lots of mascara. She must know that call sign Romeo is here to meet her, over.'

'Romeo, I would not expect anything less,' I chirped up.

'Zero, roger the description, don't forget we have guests, over.' Steve reminded us of the headquarters staff presence at the operations room.

The description of the girl's route continued:

'Echo One at blue four-two towards green one-four.'

'Zero, roger, that's Echo One towards green one-four. Romeo acknowledge.'

'Romeo, roger, I'm off comms.'

This last transmission meant that the girl was just out of sight around the corner from me. I would no longer be speaking to anyone on the radio unless it was an absolute emergency. I would continue to monitor what was going on through my earpiece, though.

As I approached the corner there was a call from one of the surveillance team to the effect that the girl was crossing the road and was about twenty metres from me. As I turned the corner and said hello to her she literally leapt in the air, turned around and ran like Linford Christie back up the road. Maybe she did not want to meet!

There were a lot of radio transmissions from various cover team members giving exact details of her route, and a few seconds later the report came in that she was in the doorway of her workplace looking back down the road towards my location. I decided to abort the operation there and then, and told all the call signs that they should make their way as planned back to the detachment office. I asked the boss if this was OK and he agreed. Everyone then clambered back into their vehicles and returned by their own routes. The helicopter returned to base and the QRF was thanked for its help and stood down, no doubt extremely disappointed about the lack of gunfights. On return to base I met the boss and the two head shed staff from headquarters. We went through the whole task debrief and then went to the bar and had a few beers. This, however, was not to be the end of this little saga.

The girl had by now been in touch with the local Sinn Fein office. They had in turn gone through their usual public relations charade, and had also complained to police head-quarters, which in turn informed the Special Branch office, which I think was just as annoyed as Sinn Fein appeared to be. Luckily for me my back was covered, and the bosses of the organisation I worked for did the right thing and informed the Branch that it was a last-minute attempt at a recruitment, and that if the opportunity had not been taken then it might not have pre-sented itself again. The local republican press then made quite a big thing about the business of the money in the cigarette packet, which came as a bit of a surprise, because as far as we were concerned the girl still had it. The sum of money was reported incorrectly. The girl claimed that she had thrown it back at us. Some days later the telephone number on the packet appeared painted on a wall in an extremely republican little village close to the border, with a bold message asking anyone who wanted to be a tout for the army to phone this particular number, although the last digit had been incorrectly transcribed.

We had a quick chat about this among ourselves. It was generally thought that if the unit was being indirectly publicised as a source-recruiting agency, then people who might want to pass information might as well have the correct details. Funnily enough, within a few evenings the number on the wall had been corrected, by a few budding painters and decorators from our detachment.

Some people living in nationalist areas where members of a terrorist persuasion hide out are sometimes prompted to vo-lunteer information about their activities when they are pre-sented with a method of doing so. Not all their neighbours are supporters of their cause. We received a number of telephone calls over a period of months, some hoax, some genuine. Matching human source information with other intelligence-gathering methods sometimes corroborates knowledge that can lead to the successful completion of what may initially have seemed to have been an unproductive operation. The fight to gain intelligence to combat terrorism, by a number of avenues, is relentless.

Chapter 8

The Recruitment

One of the most amusing characters I had dealings with, and funnily enough one of the more successful sources we ran, was a man who came to our attention owing to his friendly attitude to the troops at the various checkpoints along the border. Declan, like many people in the Province, seemingly hadn't a care in the world — he was a happy-go-lucky bloke who had a ruddy, roguish look about him. He was in his forties but looked a lot older, which might have had something to do with his clothes. He always wore a battered old suit over a recycled pullover which he'd never take off, even in the height of summer. He was an extremely likeable bloke who amused me immensely. I got along easily with him. He was also regarded with mild affection by some extremely well-known and thoroughly documented Provisional terrorists living in his home area. They very loosely trusted him, and were quite happy to give him run-of-the-mill tasks to carry out, which he did, mainly under our guidance. He loved the situation. He was, in his eyes, very important to the IRA, and in turn he was also important to us. Some of the information he supplied undoubtedly prevented one possible terrorist killing.

His recruitment into our organisation came about from his being involved in several conversations with one of our detachment collators, who had spent several days a week working out of the area that Declan would pass through on his day-to-day business. The collator would speak to him on a frequent basis. Any traffic travelling along this particular route was regularly monitored – the people in the area were known to be sympathetic to the nationalist cause, and because of this incidents recorded in the locality were high. Foot patrols of both the regular army battalions and the UDR had in the past been shot at by terrorist snipers from across the border.

During one particular spell prior to Declan's recruitment I had gone there myself for a few days, and had spent my time working with some Scottish infantry soldiers on patrols and chatting to members of the local community. Their attitude to normal people passing through their patch was not exactly what I considered to be conducive to good public relations, and it was no surprise that some terrorist had decided to organise a few snipings. They were downright offensive to the local population, who in turn hated them with a vengeance. I spoke to their Intelligence Officer on the subject in some depth, and tried to get him to encourage his lads to at least tone down their obvious hatred of anyone they considered to be a 'Teague' or a 'Fenian'. This constant barrage of abuse did absolutely nothing for us, as the whole business of approaching someone and persuading them to pass information depended on the ability to get friendly with them and establish a rapport. A difficult enough task at the best of times, it was almost impossible after they had been the subject of verbal abuse by a bunch of Glasgow Rangers supporters dressed up in British Army uniform. The bias of Protestant Scots against ordinary Northern Ireland folk within republican areas was a real problem. Historically the animosity ran very deeply in both countries.

After my little chat with the Intelligence Officer he spoke to his soldiers and for a short time at least the lads concerned did in fact tone down their negative attitude towards people passing through. On a later visit I found that they were sometimes being quite civil, but maybe it was an act for my benefit. The corporal in charge of the section and I had a brief conversation about it all. He eventually came round to accepting that what I was saying was quite relevant. It was all to do with public relations and the ability of the local people to feel they could speak freely without being harassed. If we were to get anywhere with the locals I needed his help.

Soldiers are funny creatures and have a great mistrust of anything that is slightly alien to them. Operators from our own unit, and indeed anyone from a covert background, were often treated with great suspicion. The plain fact is that soldiers do not like having you invading their space and upsetting the routine of their normal daily life. At that particular area it was assumed that if operators turned up in civilian clothes, with unshaven faces and long hair, carrying a selection of foreign automatic weapons, then there was obviously something spectacular about to go down within the next few minutes. Quite understandable, I suppose. What they did not appreciate was that by the nature of our job this could happen at any time, during any task we were involved in. It is something you accept without really dwelling on the consequences too deeply, otherwise you would end up a gibbering wreck and not get anything done. We sometimes worked alone in locations that were considered 'hard areas', places where normal soldiers would never venture unless they were part of a heavily armed patrol. The threat of attack for us was always there.

Declan, it transpired, had been travelling back and forth quite regularly through this particular area for many years, and yet none of the soldiers patrolling the area had ever contemplated getting any information out of him; it was not their job, so why bother? Our collator had been into the local intelligence cell and had been reading their daily incident reports. They consisted of a daily log of activity in the area and general comments on individual people whom the soldiers had spoken to during the course of their duties. Declan had often appeared in the log, and was noted as being very friendly, always asking if the lads went drinking and chasing the local women in the pubs in the area after they had finished work. He was interested in all the different types of weapons they carried and the number of soldiers that were likely to be in the area at any one time, and he always asked where they were from and where they were based. All classic reconnaissance-type questions of a nature likely to have a devious intent.

Not contained in those intelligence summaries were a few points that were of extreme interest to our unit, which should have been made plain by the troops right from the beginning, but the soldiers had their own selfish reasons for not including certain details. It had been brought out in conversation with the Scottish corporal that Declan supplied the soldiers with the odd bottle of poteen, and he would often pick up cigarettes and newspapers for the troops. On his way through he would be quite happy to pass the contraband from his car under the pretext of having a simple chat with the soldiers. Any people passing would just assume he was being hassled by the troops. In our estimation Declan was either involved in scouting missions for intelligence-gathering, or he was a source-recruiter's dream come true. Maybe it was a bit of both.

One of the collators and I set aside a few days a week when we would go to the area. The plan was hopefully to make contact with Declan. We knew he had a fairly regular pattern of life and we were bound to come across him sooner or later. The troops were not happy – they were aware of our reason for being there and became quite uncooperative when they realised that we had an interest in their 'delivery boy'. We met and spoke to him on a number of occasions over the next few days, and got along well from the start. He was always very amiable. On one occasion, when neither of us was there to speak to him, he noticed our absence, and asked the troops about us. We had at least made some kind of impact – he apparently made some very favourable comments about us and the way we had spoken to him. The corporal whom I had spoken with at length had continued the same line of chat with Declan, and they started to get on very well. He, at least, had actually come around to our way of approaching people, and was later to attempt to pass the selection process for our unit. As far as I know he is still serving there.

On returning the following week, and after being briefed on the latest conversations by the Scottish corporal, I decided that I would make an attempt to recruit Declan on his next drive through, hopefully that day. This was too good an opportunity to miss. I phoned the boss back at the detachment and gave him full details of what had happened and a rundown of the content of the various conversations that had taken place while the collator and I had been away. After a quick chat he gave me the go-ahead to proceed with the recruitment as I saw fit. We still had to run our operations under the Headquarters Northern Ireland guidelines, and so the exercise in umbrella coverage had to be maintained. The boss had to phone the head shed and explain what was happening.

Within an hour Declan had driven into the area. He looked genuinely pleased to see both me and the collator back on the scene. During our conversation he mentioned that we had been a bit sneaky with him, and that the corporal had told him we were different. He had quizzed the corporal on this comment and had asked how we were different, and what exactly it was we did that made us different from normal soldiers. I told him that we could probably have a better discussion over a few drinks one night, and that we should make an arrangement there and then to meet for a few beers. He became a little withdrawn at this invitation – not the usual cocky, confident Declan. He eventually said that he would go for a beer and a chat, but asked where we would meet, adding that he was quite aware that I would probably not go into the bars and pubs that he would normally frequent. After a fairly lengthy chat I convinced him that I had a number of options in mind, and would be more than happy to arrange a get-together out of sight of normal soldiers and the general public. He wanted me to explain to him there and then where I could possibly meet him, and was clearly anxious that there might be people who knew him who might see us together.

I told him that this was not a problem as we had plenty of places we could use to meet. He was obviously quite shocked to hear this and asked a lot of questions about it. He particularly stressed that he would not want to be seen by anyone other than the collator and myself. I agreed totally with him. In fact I stressed in turn that I did not particularly want to be seen in public with him either, and that he should leave it to me to make the final arrangements. This was to lead to a scenario that could have been considered an amusing situation, but with potentially disastrous results.

Declan was briefed in detail on how I would require him to drive into the area alone at an exact time the following evening. When he had been pulled over, he would be told where to go by the only soldier who would speak to him. No one else would be near the conversation. This would be one of our operators, whom he would not recognise, but he was to follow the instructions he was given implicitly. He looked quite awestruck by my briefing. He agreed to the plan and drove away with a big grin on his face. My first thought was that he was probably off to his home area to brief his terrorist masters about what he had got himself into, and that I had just arranged a potentially dangerous reactive situation for myself. This was our job, however.

The following day I arrived early at the detachment office and set about putting the operation together. The general plan took about two hours using a tried and tested format for these types of task. The old adage of the seven Ps, Prior Planning and Preparation Prevents Piss-Poor Performance, never fails. I discussed the general approach with the boss when he came in later, and I gave the rest of the operators involved the necessary full briefing. Declan had been told that he would be stopped and spoken to by one of our men and not one of the regular soldiers. He would then be given further instructions as to where he was to go and what he was to do. He must carry out his given instructions to the letter. The operator on the ground would emphasise this to him after he had been stopped. Declan's part was quite simple; our operator's role would be a lot more significant.

During the task I would appear to be working alone, but with plenty of well-hidden back-up. Declan knew me reasonably well by now and would probably assume that I would be working with a team – he would not, however, be aware of exactly how many operators there would be on the ground in the area of the operation. The task would be carried out in a slick and professional manner with the absolute minimum of activity being brought to anyone's attention. When the operation took place any people in the immediate area would not have realised what had just happened right under their noses. The plan was to then drive back to the detachment and start the process of instructing Declan on how we wanted him to give us information regarding any terrorist activities he was aware of and report to us the movements of any terrorists that he was involved with personally. It would mean that from now on he would be on our payroll, and that he should start to limit his friendly relations with the regular army troops – his errand-running days were to be slowly wound down and eventually to stop altogether. We could not afford too much attention to be drawn to his activities – he had been lucky in the past not to have been compromised.

Declan had been told to enter the area at seven o'clock precisely the following evening. If for some strange reason he could not do this, he was briefed to phone a number I had given him from a call-box. This telephone was in our operations room. He would be given an alternative time to make his drive through. If he could not get to a telephone box then he was to drive through the designated route exactly one hour later and continue with the process. I would be there. He was also briefed that if he had to use the call-box he was to make sure he was out of earshot of any third parties – this was plain common sense and was for his own safety. He accepted this quite happily and seemed to acknowledge the reasoning behind it.

At seven o'clock precisely my team were all deployed in their positions. All had reported their locations to the operations room and were awaiting the radio message from the operator who would hopefully have the first physical contact with Declan. We expected to hear a quick, straightforward transmission to the effect that the subject was through his area and heading to where we were positioned.

Every member of the team carried their own personal weapon, a Browning 9mm automatic pistol. In addition to this basic requirement all of us carried a Heckler and Koch 5.56mm machinegun with folding stock, spare magazines, smoke grenades and first-aid packs. The possible dangers of a new-source recruitment are unknown, and this operation was being carried out only a short distance from an area where we knew that the Provisionals had carried out attacks on previous occasions. All the firearms and equipment that the team carried were hidden well out of sight but could easily be brought into action in a split second, if required.

Fifteen minutes had passed and there was no sign of Declan. No calls had been made to the phone number I had given him, and so I pushed the radio pressed switch. 'All call signs, this is Romeo. Go mobile, return to your start locations at twenty hundred hours. All call signs confirm. Over.' All the team came up individually and confirmed that they had received the message and were driving out of the area.

I jumped into the front of the vehicle with the driver, another operator who was also my close cover man for the task. He looked at me, grinned, and in a mickey-taking manner said that he didn't think that this meeting was going to happen. I must say I had a doubt or two myself but, trying to be the eternal optimist, I told him that I thought he was talking out of his arse. We headed to a small, mainly Protestant village a few miles away, where we we knew we could lay up in reasonable safety away from the meeting point for a while. The village had a police station in the middle of the main street which housed a number of troops from the local battalion. I nipped out of the vehicle and went into their operations room and told them that we were in the area and that we were parked up at the front of their building but on the opposite side of the road. At least it would keep the man on guard duty happy knowing that we were 'friendly' and not a threat, which, considering our looks and dress, we could easily be taken for. This village had one or two useful attributes — a decent pub and, particularly relevant this evening, the chip shop in the main street. This was virtually the front room of someone's house, and the only thing they ever served was sausage and chips, so not exactly being spoilt for choice, we had sausage and chips.

Half an hour had passed and so, with as much speed as we could muster, we headed back to the locations we had been in previously. The team chattered away on the radio, informing each other of their chosen routes back into the area.

The boss's voice came up on the radio from our operations room. He informed us that a report had come in from a COT to the west of our position, stating that they believed they had observed unidentified armed men moving around approximately one kilometre to their east. That would make their position very close to us. I toyed with the idea of aborting the operation, but decided against it. They were unable to give any more information but would try to keep us fully informed of any new developments. My adrenalin level shot through the roof, and just for my own peace of mind I checked that each of my weapons, the Browning pistol and the Heckler and Koch, were ready. I gently released the safety catch and pulled back the cocking slide on the pistol and saw the glint of brass in the chamber. I knew it was loaded, but I had to check anyway. Everyone else on the job probably did exactly the same. Declan was really an unknown quantity. I sat in my vehicle and thought of the consequences of a set-up. I made sure that the interior light was switched off and gently eased the door open. If I had to get away quickly that would be one obstacle less to deal with.

I slowly brought the Heckler and Koch up from my side and laid it across my lap. I had trained with it hundreds of times, but as I sat there I thumbed the safety catch on and off in anticipation of the worst. My eyes were all over the place – looking in front, checking the rear-view mirror, glancing to both sides in an awkward way, straining to catch sight of any movement around me in the dusk. I quietly whistled to myself, something I had always done when I knew things were not quite right. It was my way of letting myself know I was nervous.

At five minutes past eight I decided it was pointless hanging around. I came back on the radio and told all the team to lift off and return to the detachment, the task was aborted. On the way back several arrangements were made over the radio to meet up at a pub in town where we went occasionally. After dropping off my Heckler and Koch at our arms store I quickly nipped into the operations room to book out and then jumped into my car and headed out of camp towards town. The Browning pistol, as well as two spare magazines, as always, stayed with me.

The boss had told me over the radio that he was going for a beer in town as well, so we could have a quiet chat about Declan and his non-appearance. The pub was in the middle of town and was mostly frequented by Protestants and therefore was considered fairly safe to socialise in as far as we were concerned. That particular evening there were some members of the UDR together with a few policemen and one or two faces from the local Special Branch, who, on seeing us, turned their heads or put their faces in their beer, something we were quite used to by now.

I was in the middle of a whispered conversation with the boss concerning the ins and outs of the task when Lofty, one of the other members of the team, came up and nudged me in the side. He looked at me and laughingly said that I would never guess who had just walked in. I cringed and looked at the door, expecting the worst, and there sure enough with a big grin on his face stood Declan. My very own pet leprechaun. Was this man an idiot or what? He strolled over to me quite blatantly and stood there waving his hands all over the place, apologising for not being on time at the drive-through; he had thought that to make amends he would come searching the pubs in town for me. Apparently he had been to four others before descending on this place. He proceeded to explain that a friend's cow was just about to calve and that he was a dab hand at delivering them and that he had completely forgotten the time. I looked at him intently, stared at him at eye level, and gently told him that this really was not a good fucking idea at all and he should get out of the pub, go home directly and I would speak to him at some stage during the following day.

He could tell that I was more than just a little bit annoyed about his appearance by the tone of my voice, and he made a hasty retreat to the door. The problem for us now was that there was the very real possibility of a welcoming committee from an IRA ASU outside the place, waiting to give us the good news. Declan knew exactly what we looked like, what we were wearing and, more to the point, could easily sit back and identify us to a potential gunman. He could have been telling the truth, but this was a dangerous business and the possible threat of an attack had to be taken seriously.

I popped upstairs and phoned our operations room. Luckily for us two of the lads involved with the evening's activities were still at the detachment, writing up their orders for a similar operation to be carried out over the following weekend. I gave them a quick brief on what had happened and asked them to cover the pub carpark and watch us out. I also asked the duty operator to phone the checkpoint and told him to page me when Declan had been reported going back through their position and was safely out of harm's way on his way home. I returned to the bar and had a quick chat with the boss and the other lads. The message from the checkpoint came through on my vibrating message pager about twenty minutes later. It was confirmed that Declan had passed through the area and was nowhere near our location any more. One of the other operators and I then headed out to the carpark. It was packed, and I could not see either of my two colleagues. I was, however, quite happy that they would be there hidden away somewhere, covering us out. Within a few minutes all the other members of our detachment had left the pub, and we all headed in different directions through the town away from the area. The pub now had an out-of-bounds status imposed on it for a while.

Early the following morning, along with the collator, I made my way to the area that I knew Declan would definitely be passing through at some stage during the day. I eventually met him at about two o'clock that afternoon and had to restrain myself from knocking his head off because of the little stunt he had pulled the previous evening. I gave him a verbal hammering and explained that he had already made a very stupid move and we had not yet discussed exactly why I wanted to meet him, although he had a good idea. He had realised what a mistake he had made, and after the bollocking was given I played the situation down because I did not want to scare him off at this very early stage. We once again went into the instructions I had previously briefed him on, and after I was happy that he would carry them out to the letter I let him go on his way. I phoned the detachment, gave the boss the brief details of my conversation with Declan, and then made my way back to give the same set of orders as had been passed the night before. There were a few light-hearted comments from the lads at the briefing about how maybe we should tell Declan where we operated from and get him to come straight here, saving us the problem of mounting a job, and maybe he could bring some poteen for us as well!

One of our collators had been asked by the boss to go to the COT office that had reported the armed men the night before to get an update and speak to their controller. He spoke to the officer concerned and took a look at the UDR's part-timers' patrol sheet from that evening. Lo and behold, they had a patrol in the area at the very same time and at exactly the grid reference where the report had mentioned the sighting of possible armed men. Luckily enough for both parties none of us had met up. It would have been an extremely embarrassing fuck-up for all concerned – there could have been a classic 'blue on blue' situation where someone could have been killed by our own troops. Against my usual instincts it was decided to impose one of our rarely placed 'out of bounds' on the army, police or UDR patrolling that same night in the area where we would be working. At least then if there was a report of any armed men, or sightings by our team of such activity, we could assume it was a worst-case scenario. At seven o'clock precisely my earpiece burst into life.

'All calls, this is Alpha. Tango One through our location and heading towards you and is clear.'

I immediately pressed the radio pressel in the back of the vehicle and acknowledged the message. All the other call signs involved did the same to confirm that they were aware of the situation. Tango One was the call sign we had allocated to Declan. The last piece of information stating that he was clear meant that in the operator's opinion he was not under any form of surveillance and that we should continue with the job. No sausage and chips tonight!

The next transmission I heard over the radio was from the first cover car. He had carried out his part of the operation and was informing me that Declan had performed his drills as he had been briefed. Other members of the team were joining in the radio commentary when they became part of the task. When an operation like this is under way it is essential that the real-time observations of the operators are transmitted as they are made. In the case of an emergency it is paramount that everyone knows what the exact situation is.

The operation went smoothly and Declan was impressed. It is

vital in our work that this is exactly the impression given to the source. We were, after all, ensuring his safety as well as our own. Any sloppy tradecraft from us could mean that he would lose faith in us or, at worst, be dead within a very short time.

With Declan safely on board we were driven by one of my team members to a debriefing room containing a comfortable three-piece suite, a coffee table and some pieces of furniture and pictures to at least try to provide a relaxed atmosphere in which we could speak to the sources. I had produced some cigarettes and a few cans of beer from one of the cupboards. This, after all, was to be the social meeting I had told him I would arrange for us. He seemed impressed again and settled down to a few hours' chat with me on a variety of subjects concerning his contacts and associates along with their habits and routines. He was very enthusiastic. I needed to check the ownership of a variety of vehicle registration numbers he had given me and had to leave the room. I left him with a few newspapers and magazines to look at and told him I would be about fifteen minutes and that he should make himself comfortable.

On my return he had obviously just dashed back to his chair. He sat there looking as innocent as he possibly could. He had been snooping around, and why not – I would have done exactly the same if I were in his position. I asked him if he fancied another beer, to which he emphatically answered that he did not and that he really must be heading home. I think he had been embarrassed when I had returned to the room. He turned down the offer of more cigarettes as well. We finished off the initial debrief and made arrangements for his next meeting with me for the following week. I gave him a few easy tasks to carry out for me in between. He assured me he would try and undertake these to the best of his ability. He apologised profusely to me for his various indiscretions. It was actually quite hilarious watching him squirm.

Over a number of years Declan came to us with some steady information. His credibility was considered to be in doubt at times by our headquarters because he was regarded as a scallywag. He would tell us about his thieving of sheep from farms and a multitude of other petty crimes. He even tried selling me some forged Irish punts at one stage. Along with my partner, who was co-handling the case, I decided it was about time Declan really started to work for his money. We encouraged him to join Sinn Fein, deliver leaflets, go to meetings and generally get known as sympathetic to their cause. We often told him that it would be very nice if he came up with some extremely useful information that could be used to good effect. We encouraged him to get friendly with known Provisional terrorists in his area and get himself trusted by them. He assured us that he was trying to improve his access and that he would surprise us in the very near future. One night he certainly did.

I was lounging about at home one evening when the duty operator rang me. The message he had to pass was that 'Terry', which was Declan's telephone nickname, had rung to say that he was just about to come into our area and he had 'a long' with him. This was the nickname we had briefed him to use to describe the length of a weapon. He also said that he was only going to have it in his possession for a few more hours, and if we needed to see it then we had better arrange something very quickly. He would ring the detachment back in twenty minutes to find out what was required of him. I told the duty operator to ring the boss at home and ask him to make his way to the detachment. I also told him to ring the specialist intelligence unit that dealt with weapons and find out if they wanted to be involved in this or not, and that when Declan rang back to inform him that we would see him at 'Dougie's pub' at nine o'clock. 'Dougie's pub' meant nothing at all relating to our immediate area − it referred to a little pub I had come across when I had been fishing one day on a river several miles to the east of where we worked, and was a code word for one of the emergency routes that Declan had been briefed on. There was not going to be enough time to get everyone from their houses into the detachment for a full set of orders, so I decided to quickly phone two of the operators and give them a quick rundown of the required task over the telephone. I mentioned to each of them that any other information that was needed could be passed over the radio on the way to pick up the source.

We had all worked together on a number of similar tasks over a period of a few years. We all knew the routes inside out, and were all very aware of what was required should a problem arise. What I had completely failed to remember was that Declan had not actually been through the route I had told him to be on. 'Dougie's pub' was going to be his initiation into the world of emergency meetings; this was his first 'fast ball'. He had been briefed on it a number of times and had run through it mentally with me on a few occasions to confirm he knew what was required. It meant he had to drive through a town in the north of our area and reach a point about three miles south from there at the designated time. He would see my car somewhere on that route and we would go from there. That basically was his full brief. What he was never fully informed of was the end location and which way we were likely to lead him after the pick-up had been completed. This was obviously a general safety point for ourselves and allowed a decent period of time for the cover team to ensure that he was not being followed into the area of the operation. I was aware from the message that he was going to be extremely pushed for time tonight, and so very hurriedly I tried to make arrangements with the operations room for the weapons people to meet us at a place where I had previously carried out a reconnaissance for just this type of call – a thickly wooded area on the shore of the lough some miles to our north. They could wait for me to turn up with the 'long' that Declan was bringing along with him. As this was all being arranged over the radio I was heading like a bat out of hell along the road from my house to be at 'Dougie's pub' on time. It was now approaching fifteen minutes to nine. I looked at my speedometer — it was flickering between 100 and 110 miles per hour. I hoped that I was not going to be caught at a police vehicle checkpoint on the way. The other two operators on the task lived nearer to the plot than I did and were in the area already. They had told me over the radio that they had swept the locality looking for any suspicious vehicles or people. In their opinion everything seemed to be clear. That was good enough for me.

I positioned myself off the road just about a mile or so to the south of the start of the journey that Declan would be taking. By now he should have been nearly approaching the start point of his route, where one of the operators would give a live commentary on his movements. The boss came on the radio to say that the weapons unit people had been called to a more important weapons find in one of the cities, and asked that we should take extensive details of the weapon, photograph it if possible, and inform them of all these details at a later date. I thought, fucking brilliant.

We had been laid up at the area for about a quarter of an hour when the detachment operations room came up on the radio saying that Declan was on the telephone and wanted to know where I was. The request had me pausing for a few seconds — not a single car had passed us since we had been in position. After thinking that maybe we had missed him or that maybe he had driven through earlier than arranged, I asked them to find out exactly where he was. They came back to me again and stated that he was looking for 'Dougie's pub'. The radio operator's voice stressed the name. As they said this with such

Clearing and checking a weapon contained in a terrorist cache. This particular weapon is a derivative of the Kalashnikov AK series and was in perfect working condition. Note the hessian sacks laid for lessening ground sign and the medical gloves for weapon handling.

The deadly contents of a terrorist weapons hide. All these weapons were in perfect working order and were clean and well oiled ready for use. Note the ammunition magazines at the far end.

Another range training day. The weapon being used here is the Heckler & Koch HK553. This was my personal choice for use as a support weapon whilst working on operations in the Province. It has a phenomenal rate of fire and is very dependable.

A colleague uses an unorthodox position by holding the magazine whilst firing, it does however allow rapid changing to a fresh magazine when the ammunition runs out.

The moment of truth. Operators checking their targets for hits at the 'butts'. The standard of weapon handling and marksmanship was very high.

Myself and one of the women at the detachment run through a series of safety drills prior to live firing. The women are trained in CQB and weapon handling as equally as the male operators.

One of the many articles that appeared in the local republican press following a recruitment attempt carried out by the detachment on a local female.

Girl hitch-hiker "offered bribe by British Intelligence" claim

MEMBERS of British Intelligence, travelling in a private car, bearing a Dublin licence plate, are alleged to have offered a young female hitch-hiker from   a bribe in return for information about certain people in the   area.

The girl, who is employed in   rejected the offer of money in £20 notes stuffed inside an empty cigarette carton, and ignored a request to ring a cetrain number the following day.

The incident, related by the girl, who does not wish to be named, has been condemned by Sinn Fein Councillor, Mr.   whose area borders on   and with whom the frightened girl made contact.

" I regard this as a very serious occurrence in so far as these people were driving around in a 1987 Dublin registered car and they openly identified themselves as members of British Intelligence and it would appear they had nothing to do with the RUC or the UDR."

Cllr.   said the girl, after being propositioned, had asked the driver to stop the car so that sh could get out.

" The refusal to do so amounted to abduction," claimed Cllr.

The girl says her ordeal began as she thumbed her way into work last week. She was a short distance from the permanent British Army checkpoint at   on the Enniskillen road.

A car with Dublin registration plates pulled up and inside was a male driver with a female passenger. The girl got in.

Shortly after the car had moved off heading for Enniskillen, the driver told the girl her name.

She denied she was that person, but he persisted and claimed he knew all about her.

According to Cllr.   whom the girl also told her story to, the man introduced himself as " Geoff" and his female companion as " Cass."

" He said they were members of British Intelligence and they wanted to get some information about a number of people in the   area."

The girl, at this stage frightened by the experience, asked the driver to stop the car, but her request was ignored. She tried to open her door, but it was locked.

" She was asked to make contact with them that evening. She said that was impossible and they then asked her to make contact the following evening after work. The man repeated his desire to talk about a number of people in the   area, but when the girl asked who these people were, she was told there wasn't enough time at that stage; however, there would be more

time the following day," said Cllr.

CIGARETTE PACKET

By this stage the car had arrived in Enniskillen, where the driver, before getting out to let the girl out, passed her a cigarette box.

" It had her full name on it and a note, ' Ring Geoff,' quoting a telephone number, and while she was opening the door, the girl flipped the packet and saw that the inside was stuffed with £20 notes. As soon as she got out of the car she threw the packet back in, saying ' You can keep that. I don't want anything to do with that.' "

Too frightened to go into work, the girl returned home, and from there contacted Cllr.   who, in turn, advised her to contact her local elected representative.

Meanwhile, as the girl — as was her habit — walked from work the next day to the bus depot, the driver of the car from the previous day called to her from across the street. She immediately took fright and ran back to where she worked.

Cllr.   said at the week-end that the actions of the people in the car had placed the girl's job in jeopardy.

" She may not be able to continue to go to work in   and, altogether, it's a very serious thing that a young girl should be harassed like that, on her own, at 9 o'clock in the morning," he said.

It is understood that the girl has since contacted a solicitor about the matter.

(Above) During the funeral procession of IRA man Kevin Brady, two British army corporals were ruthlessly murdered. The actions of the killers at the event led to the recruitment of one of the FRU's best agents from the republican community.

(Left) Clearing the undergrowth away from the location of a potential weapons hide. Bobby traps were always a possibility when undertaking these types of operations.

This particular hide contained two hand guns, a pistol and a revolver, which had been covered in a thick waterproof plastic covering to maintain their working order.

Car drills were an essential part of continuation training. One operator gives covering fire for his colleague as he moves back to a position and takes up a firing position himself. The firing operator will then move away from the vehicle. This movement is known as 'pepper-potting'.

Two operators make good use of the vehicle to give them cover from enemy fire. Once the initial firing has taken place they will take up the 'pepper-potting' routine to get away from the area.

The result of some over-enthusiastic car drills.

An operator from the unit in heavy disguise.

Helicopters are an absolute necessity for carrying out reconnaissance tasks and surveillance, they also provide a medical evacuation means of transport which is second-to-none. Myself and one of our pilots pose in front of his Gazelle helicopter prior to flying out on a task.

The detachment line-up just prior to my departure from the unit. The faces have all changed but the weaponry and firepower still remains the same.

London. The IRA bomb which exploded at Staples Corner went off as I was driving towards the area. The crater left by the seat of the explosion under the elevated section can be clearly seen.

Northern Ireland. Not all the activities in the Province are terrorist orientated. Fishing was my escape from my role in the detachment.

The gentle surface ripple on a mountain lough. The perfect end to the perfect day.

conviction, I had this terrible thought. Fucking hell, no – Declan had driven south-east and was looking for the real place of that name. During my brief to him some time earlier he had mentioned that he had come across the name of that particular pub but had never been there, I had stressed to him at the time that it was just a nickname. It was about thirty-five miles to our east, and even on a very clear road it would mean driving like a madman to get there within about three-quarters of an hour. I asked the operations room just to confirm with Declan again and told them to forget any telephone security procedures; just ask him precisely where he was. My worst thoughts were confirmed. The fact that we were using the name as a code name for something completely different had gone straight in one ear, tumbled about in the sawdust and then had shot out again like Thrust Two up the desert.

I told the operations room to tell him to stay exactly where he was and to wait for us to arrive. In the meantime could they inform one of our other detachments in that area about the situation and get one of their operators to drive up there and take a look for us. As we approached the area just over forty minutes later, the operator from the other detachment came on the radio and told me that I would not believe what he was just about to tell me. I replied, 'Try me, over.' Declan was standing in the middle of the roundabout just down the road from the pub, drunk as a skunk, leaning on what appeared to be a weapon of some sort. How he was never shot by a passing patrol I will never know. The weapon turned out to be a shotgun. How I kept my hands from wringing his neck that night still baffles me. He was completely pissed out of his mind and hardly recognised me.

He told me he had been pushed into doing something like this to keep us happy. I had kept telling him that he was being paid good money for working with us, and he should be making more effort with his tasking. I took the gun away from him and placed it in the boot of his car. I then gave him the choice of sleeping it off in the vehicle or of making some kind of arrangement to get him home. He fell about the place and I decided to leave him there. He was last seen spread out like a bag of rags over his back seat.

The next time we met up I impressed upon him that it was real information and real equipment that we needed to get our hands on, and that his little stunt had nearly dropped me in the shit with my headquarters. He seemed genuinely concerned about this and promised faithfully that he would not pull a stunt like that again. The drinking had started him thinking of stupid ways he could impress me, and that was why he had contacted me. I had earlier been slagging off the specialist weapons team for not being around for the meeting to do their part of the business with the weapon we were collecting. Believe me, I was extremely glad that they had not wasted their journey. My embarrassment level would have gone through the roof and it would have cost me a lot in beer in recompense.

One evening Declan telephoned the detachment asking to bring forward his usual weekly meeting with me to that day, twenty-four hours early, as he had some very important information for me. He said it was essential that we met. From his conversation I could tell that he had not been drinking and he really did need to speak to me urgently. I gave him a route to walk and told him what time he should start out. As I approached to pick him up I noticed that he had an urgent look about him I had not seen before. This intrigued me, and I was looking forward to hearing what he had to say.

I took him to a quiet lane, and before I had had a chance to start the routine of making sure the team were happy that there was no surveillance or hostile third parties around, he told me that he knew about someone who was to be killed that week. I told him to hang on until we had made our way to the debriefing area and I would get all the details then. I parked up, and even before I had switched the engine off he immediately launched into a burst of high-speed speech that I found hard to understand. I encouraged him to relax, slow down and very gradually tell me everything he knew. He then explained to me that as usual he was in a certain pub earlier in the day, although he stressed that he had not touched a drink – this was where he reckoned most of the area's known IRA people went drinking. This I knew was quite true – the bar was noted for its clientèle of Provisionals. It had also been reported by other informants that discussions in this bar were sometimes quite open about the activities of the Provisionals, although consisting mainly of historic information, and usually as a form of 'back-slapping' if one of their operations against the security forces in Northern Ireland had gone to plan.

Declan said that he had definitely overheard a conversation between two men in motor bike leathers relating to a part-time officer in the Ulster Defence Regiment who was to be shot as he left his home later that week. The man concerned was quite well known locally and was very outspoken against the IRA and its cause. Over the years he had made himself a public figure and he was well known to a number of Provisionals who lived close to him. They had already watched his movements and had carried out their own equivalent of a pattern-of-life survey to find out when he would be in the best possible place for them to be able to kill him. They had decided to shoot him as he left home early one morning, either on Thursday or Friday. Declan really put the icing on the cake and convinced me that it was real information when he stated the officer's full name and told me exactly where he lived. This was completely outside his usual area of knowledge. He almost appeared to be scared as he imparted the information, not exhibiting his usual relaxed attitude to life at all.

Headquarters Northern Ireland was informed of the situation and so was the local Special Branch office. In a quickly arranged meeting between the various command elements of the security forces, it was decided that a reactive attack could not be carried out. The SAS troop was already deployed at another location and they did not want to leave the job to any other agency. It was decided that the officer in question should be informed of the possible attack and that he should be allowed to contribute his own ideas as well as being advised as to what we believed he should do. The officer had been the subject of two previous attempts on his life and took the whole thing rather casually. He informed my boss that he would simply go away on holiday earlier than he had intended, and that hopefully would throw the Provisionals plans again this time. As he said himself, the threat would always be there – it was just a matter of when it would be carried out.

The following morning he headed off to France with his wife for two weeks. No information was ever forthcoming as to whether the Provisionals had gone to the house to make the attack. Patrols of uniformed soldiers were increased in that area over the two weeks he was away, and that may have been enough to divert the attentions of the Provisionals to another plan.

There was, however, a postscript to the information we had received from Declan. A police detective living on the outskirts of the same village as the officer was shot the following week as he came out of his house. Both he and his son, also a policeman, had returned shots at their two assailants, who left the area on a motorbike. The detective was wounded, although not seriously, and the son claimed that he had certainly hit one of the attackers. No one has ever been questioned or arrested for this murder attempt.

The officer moved away from the area a few months later and

retired from the UDR soon after, although he still publicly proclaims his opinion of the Provisionals and their actions. I have no doubt that Declan's information diverted the attack on him to another target, who luckily was able to defend himself to a certain degree, and maybe even scored a success with the son's return of gunfire.

Chapter 9

The Cortège Recruitment

T he recruitment of an agent with the ability to gain access to higher levels of information on terrorists in the Province was a painstaking, dangerous process. Numerous weeks, often months, were spent searching for the character who was able to move freely within this community without suspicion, was accepted without question, and was brave enough to provide the intelligence we needed. The correct motivation was sometimes all we required for a timely recruitment attempt to be successful. Occasionally, luck played a part as well. One such person came to our attention through a series of events that provided her with the motivation we were looking for.

The day 6 March 1988 witnessed one of the most controversial events ever involving specialised British troops. It became front-page news in Britain and the rest of the world for weeks after. It also became the cause of a major uproar in Northern Ireland. A small special projects team from the SAS Regiment had some days beforehand deployed to Gibraltar, and had been involved in a surveillance task carried out on three known IRA terrorists – Danny McCann, Sean Savage and

Mairead Farrell. They were under suspicion of being in the final stages of planning a terrorist attack on Government House. Other possibilities for a terrorist offensive included the changing-of-the-guard ceremony, which would be carried out by the Royal Anglian Regiment at Ince's Hall, situated in the main street, or any number of other British military locations situated close by.

McCann was a top Provisional IRA man from the Clonard district of Belfast. His accomplices were both equally dedicated to the cause. Sean Savage was the nephew of a former IRA Belfast commander, Billy McKee. Mairead Farrell had long been associated with the republican movement. She was a convent-educated, bright and attractive woman. She was also a convicted terrorist, who had been one of the main instigators behind the women of Armagh jail joining in the dirty protest. For all three to be together in Gibraltar was understandably of great interest to British Intelligence, and it was a foregone conclusion that they would be in the process of organising some form of terrorist attack which had to be stopped.

Source information from Belfast had indicated that McCann and Savage were in possession of a large quantity of Semtex explosive, courtesy of the IRA's Libyan connections. Both of these men had a record of involvement in a variety of terrorist activities, one of the more notorious of these being the murder of three Special Branch men at the Liverpool Bar in the Belfast dockside area the previous year. Farrell was also well documented and had served a prison sentence for her involvement in the bombing campaign during the seventies. These three people were top-class terrorists.

The reactive operation carried out by the SAS soldiers was to cause a major furore. When the three suspects were shot dead it had been assumed that their terrorist attack was imminent. This would obviously have caused the deaths of a number of British soldiers, along with countless tourists who were gathered in the area to watch the guard-changing ceremony. The Enniskillen bomb had proved that the IRA had no compassion or sympathy where the deaths of innocent civilians attending military ceremonies were concerned. The SAS team took no chances, and the result was the deaths of McCann, Savage and Farrell. They were unarmed.

The follow-up investigation discovered a car in an underground carpark in Marbella near the Spanish border with Gibraltar. It was found to contain a massive amount of explosives and detonating equipment. It also contained three sets of false passports and travel documentation. The SAS team were found by the European Court of Human Rights to be blameless, even though the killings were classed as unlawful. The court found that their actions had undoubtedly saved lives.

The bodies of McCann, Savage and Farrell were taken back to Northern Ireland for burial.

Milltown Cemetery is in the republican district of Andersonstown in the south-west part of Belfast, near the Falls Road area to the west and the main M1 motorway to the east. It had become a focal point in the many years of the Troubles. This funeral was to perpetuate its notoriety further. Because of its obvious sensitivity a 'stand-off' approach had been adopted by the police and military authorities. There was no close-vicinity coverage by either the RUC or the army; there were no uniforms to be seen in close proximity to the crowd. Covert activity was kept to an absolute minimum. As the funeral ceremony got under way a number of explosions took place. A Protestant extremist named Michael Stone was seen to be running amok in the cemetery throwing grenades and firing a gun with complete disregard for the safety of the crowd. He was eventually arrested by the police, but he had left three people dead and many others injured or wounded in the wake of his violence. The funeral of one of the casualties of Stone's attack was to bring more problems, which were to shock and sicken all sections of the community and the rest of the country. Ironically, the events of that day were to bring to our detachment one of the most useful and brave sources I was to encounter in the Province during my tour. The motivation was instilled through the events that were to follow.

As the Gibraltar funerals had been so incredibly tense, it was not surprising that three days later, at the burial of one of Michael Stone's victims, Kevin Brady, the RUC and the army were kept well out of the area. As the funeral cortège proceeded along its route, the only visible sign of any military presence was a Lynx helicopter from the Army Air Corps flight at Aldergrove hovering a few thousand feet above the crowd. The funeral procession was being marshalled by the community and proceeded unimpaired on its way to the cemetery. The helicopter, nicknamed 'heli-tele', was fitted with an extremely powerful video camera. The 'heli-tele' picked up a commotion of some sort on the ground, and the camera operator followed events as best he could. It could not have been clear to the crew exactly what was going on below them at street level through their video camera monitor. Such equipment is an effective aid to surveillance but has restrictions with regard to its ability to produce instant images with enough clarity to enable an operator to provide exact details of any activity. But the incident was videotaped as the crewman followed the on-going pandemonium.

Television crews covering the funeral on the cortège route were to transmit the gruesome attack on two unidentified people who were in the process of being forcibly removed from a silver Volkswagen Passat. At one stage a single pistol shot was fired from inside the car and the crowd surged away from the immediate area. Almost immediately they reconverged on the vehicle and the two occupants were dragged out and beaten unmercifully by a crowd acting like a pack of madmen. The two occupants were bundled into, and taken away by, a black taxicab which drove at high speed through the crowds, eventually stopping at some wasteland behind shops at the rear of the Falls Road. Having been stripped and beaten half conscious they were finally executed with their own weapon, a Browning pistol. This gun clearly been seen being held aloft by one of the men, who had been trying to escape out of the driver's window of the car during the attack. A local Belfast priest, Father Alec Reid, who had apparently tried to save the men, was the last person to be seen close to them as an army patrol arrived in the area. They had been deployed as quickly as possible. Unfortunately it took them two minutes to get there and the men were already dead. The murderers had fled the area and had gone into hiding.

A short time later Headquarters Northern Ireland was to reveal that the unfortunate occupants of the vehicle were two British soldiers, Corporals Robert Howes and Derek Woods, both members of the Corps of Royal Signals. There have been many theories and much conjecture about what they were doing in the area and how they ended up being the victims of a sickening attack and murder. They were certainly not involved in any covert activity. They had been carrying out a routine check on signals equipment contained in various military locations in the area prior to Corporal Woods being posted away from the Province, which was due to happen in the following weeks.

In the area to the south of a small town situated in the far north-west corner of our area of responsibility, a uniformed patrol from the resident infantry regiment was about to call on the home of a well-known female in our patch. She was a Sinn Fein supporter and hardline republican. The female's unfavourable attitude to the troops had been quite well documented over the years. Regular house calls to this particular town by the army patrols were a purely routine part of their day, and as the patrol commander approached the woman's door he knew he would probably get very little, if any, response from her.

The rest of the patrol was told to hang around in the area of the driveway to await his return. There was no point in all of them trudging up to her doorway – she would have enough to complain about with just him there. After the commander's quick chat with the female they radioed in to the operations room for a helicopter to pick them up for their return journey to base. About an hour after they returned to camp the patrol commander called round to our detachment and asked to speak to someone concerning some information that he thought might be of use to us. It certainly was.

The female they had visited was a particularly attractive, single woman in her early thirties, who had just been watching the televised events at the Kevin Brady funeral in Belfast when the patrol had called at her home. She had apparently been crying uncontrollably when she eventually answered the door to the patrol commander, and she asked him to come into the house and tell her more about what had been going on at the funeral. She told him that she had been physically sickened by what she had seen, and that this was not her idea of how to solve the problems in Northern Ireland. She said that the men involved in this attack and those who had killed the soldiers were no better than wild animals, and that she hoped to find a way 'to do something about it'. The events she had witnessed had given her the necessary motivation we were looking for.

Another uniformed patrol was organised for later the same day during which one or two members of our detachment would visit her house. The recruitment operation would be quite simple, with Lofty doing the initial chat-up. The intention was to play on her obviously susceptible emotional state after witnessing the attack. It worked.

She turned out to be a very sensitive, thoughtful person, quite the opposite to the intelligence picture of her that had been built up over a number of years which focused on her 'hard' republican views. Her attitude to the army patrols that had called at her house had always given the impression that she could never be considered as a potential source. The day's events, however, had turned the tables for her. She was still as keen as ever to pursue the line supporting the total withdrawal of British troops from Ulster, she still wanted to see a united Ireland, but she saw no need to achieve this with terrorism and violence. As far as she was concerned these ambitions could be achieved politically, without the input of the Provisional IRA and their so-called armed struggle.

I was brought onto the new task as Lofty's co-handler. We gave the woman the cover name Brenda, although by most of the blokes within the detachment she was nicknamed 'BB', not because she bore any resemblance to Brigitte Bardot, but because she would always turn up for our covert meetings dressed as if she were on her way out to a night club or a party, with more than an ample amount of cleavage on show. To this day I'm convinced she squeezed her ample charms into a bra one size too small just for our benefit. She was an attractive woman who would wear almost tarty clothes; this, however, only increased the interest from the detachment studs, who would always try to volunteer their services when Lofty or I were due to meet her. BB, Busty Brenda, had become a detachment legend.

Brenda continued to work for the local Sinn Fein party. She was still very active in republican circles and had tremendous access to people that we were interested in in certain border areas. She was a natural who was both confident and bright; she was also a very shrewd lady. She would scour the local papers looking for events, like ceilidhs or band nights which local players were likely to attend. She'd even take her camera along and take snaps of them so we could have more up-to-date photographs from which to identify them.

Overall the detachment was beginning to make a lot of headway, and the intelligence coverage we had of this particular area was deepening on an almost daily basis. With input also from Declan, who covered a similar patch, we were starting to gather a lot of information we had previously never managed to get access to, information which was of particular interest to a number of other covert agencies. The beauty of having two human sources covering the same geographical points without knowledge of each other's activities is that it gave us the ability to cross-reference their reports. Brenda, at one of our many meetings, came out with an absolute cracker of a statement which had both Lofty and I grinning at each other behind her back. We had suggested she should start to think of other people we could approach to use in our intelligence-gathering tasks. She had proceeded to give us a full report on the fact that Declan was someone we could certainly use to gather information. Little did she realise that he had been debriefed on his own activities and had made reference to her only the evening before. She was sat in the same seat that he had occupied twenty-four hours previously.

Declan had been asked to get friendly with a known terrorist in his home town, a character named Liam Donnelly. We wanted full information on all his known habits, up-to-date details of any vehicles he drove and his close friends, his financial situation, and anything else he could possibly find out about him. Declan, in his own inimitable style, carried out his allotted task with a vengeance. We met up a few days later and he was extremely happy to inform us that he had been drinking with the individual concerned and that he had loads to tell us about him. Most of the information was very basic, but it was useful background knowledge which we could work on. However, he made a strange remark to the effect that the man in question was 'a dirty wee fucker'.

Donnelly apparently had a passion for going to singles nights at clubs in the hope of meeting women for sex. Declan informed me that the man did not care what the women looked like and was of the opinion that if they were at these clubs on these nights then they could only be after one thing as well. Maybe it was time to bring out Brenda's full potential.

Lofty and I had both been associated with Brenda for some time by this stage, and our intelligence debriefings were always very straight and to the point. She was very sharp, knew instinctively what we were after and did not seem to hold back when providing us with the information we needed. She was always more than keen to please. This latest request was going to be a bit different, though. We asked her if she had ever come across the man that Declan had given us the information on; she had heard of him. She was asked if she could go into the bars where he drank and try to get friendly with him. She looked at us knowingly and laughed out loud. She knew what we were up to and had what could only be termed as a dirty grin on her face. Without any hint of embarrassment she then asked us if we wanted her to go to bed with him. We asked if she would, and with a further laugh she stated that she was happy to get friendly with him, if we wanted her to, but the rest would have to wait until she saw him. She enjoyed the company of men, but she would probably not jump straight into the sack with him. She asked a few questions relating to the subject in hand. How did we know that Donnelly would fancy her? Why were we so certain she would be able to get near him? We explained gently that we knew he had a soft spot for the female population of the world, and that we had no reason to believe that he would turn her away given half a chance. There again, not many blokes would.

With her co-operation we came up with a ploy to 'honey-trap' the man. We asked her to find out which nightclubs ran discos for the over-thirties in his area. We would get a full description of the bloke from Declan so she could identify him, and then we would brief her on exactly how we wanted her to make contact with him. We did not want her to have a full-on relationship with Donnelly straight away – she was to play 'hard to get' and keep him at a distance until we thought he was ready for the plucking. We had unconfirmed reports from a variety of sources that he was a quartermaster for the Provisional IRA, and he was definitely wanted for questioning on a variety of offences concerning terrorist-related incidents, including one bombing several years previously and the attempted murder of a part-time member of the Ulster Defence Regiment. It was thought that he was still very active in the procurement of arms and ammunition, along with the organising of terrorist training activities.

The following week Declan informed us that the quartermaster was due to go to a nightclub on the Thursday. It was holding a 'grab a granny' night. Declan was also aware of which pub he would be going to prior to his visit to the nightclub. This would mean that he would be able to give us a detailed description of what the man was wearing. We had to be careful that Declan did not cotton on to our ploy with Brenda, and I gave him a complete 'decoy' briefing to distract him from the real reasons I wanted this detailed information. Brenda was informed of the impending disco, and we arranged to meet her prior to her night out. She was buzzing with excitement about it, and I had to reiterate a few points about not going in too strongly. The whole point was to get the man dangling on a string so that she dictated the situation, not he.

The night arrived and Lofty and I met Brenda in the early part of the evening. Fair play to her, she looked the part and was obviously looking forward to her night on the 'trap'. I had received a call from Declan, and he had given me a detailed description of what the quarry was wearing and who he was with. Brenda was briefed that she was not to make an approach to the man or speak to him. She was to position herself so that he made the approach and was to appear uninterested in his advances. From the information we had on him this would only encourage him further – he was a very determined man. If the ploy failed tonight there would be many more occasions on which we could send Brenda out. We were convinced the man would approach her at some stage. Off she went.

I received a call from Brenda the following morning. It had worked. She explained to me at a meeting later that day how she had hung around at the end of one of the bars just before closing time, in direct view of the man she knew was her target from the description we had given her. He had been unsuccessful in trapping any other female during the night and had made a direct suggestion that they should leave together and go to his place for a 'wee dram'. She had played him perfectly, and at the very last minute had disappeared out of sight, but not without giving him an address where he could write to her.

Brenda and Donnelly swapped one or two letters over the next few weeks. We dictated the content together. They had to be worded in such a way that he would not lose interest – he had to believe he was on to a good thing. She used a post office box number in the early days of the arrangement. As the liaison by mail went on, we encouraged her to make moves to meet up with him. We got her to write more intimate and personal letters – he had to be kept walking a tightrope so that he would eventually be gagging to meet her again. In her next letter she explained that she would love to get together with him. She asked him for his telephone number and suggested he might like to meet up with her for a night out. She also included a photograph of herself looking very horny; the bait worked.

We met up with Brenda the evening before she was due to meet him. She was still keen on the idea and told us that she had got a special outfit sorted for the following evening and that he would not be able to resist her. She reckoned she could have him on his knees no matter how hard a man he was. We gave her some extra money for her expenses as well as her usual source payment. She was also reminded of her reason for meeting him, and was encouraged to take it slowly and develop things at a reasonable pace. She was one of the sources who genuinely seemed embarrassed about receiving money in payment for her information, but, like all the others, she never refused.

Brenda had done the business – she had him literally eating out of the palm of her hand. Over a period of about three months she was meeting the man regularly. She inevitably started having sex with him and gave us a great deal of information about him, even supplying us with photographs of both him and his house, which were just unobtainable by other means. His out-of-date photograph appeared on the montages issued to the troops and intelligence cells of known players. He looked nothing like it, and it was no surprise when she informed us that he had been travelling back and forth into Northern Ireland for a long time completely unknown to the troops at the vehicle checkpoints. After a major incident in our area he decided to stay away as he thought he had been pushing his luck. Whether he had anything to do with the provision of the explosives for that attack is not known, but he never crossed the border after the event.

The lengthy process of gathering detailed information on Donnelly continued. Brenda informed us that he was forever disappearing for up to three weeks at a time – she never knew where. He was very cagey about his trips. He would just tell her that he had to go away on business, although she knew he did not have any kind of job. While he was out of the house on one occasion Brenda had literally turned the place over. She told us that she had searched it high and low to look for anything that might be of use or interest to us. As she was going through a set of drawers in his bedroom she had heard him coming in through the front door. Her car was in the driveway and he had not been expecting her. She told me that she whipped her clothes off and jumped straight into bed. As he walked in the room she had a large grin on her face and she 'welcomed' him home. What a woman!

Let's make no mistake. This was not a game. If Brenda's cover had been blown she would have been considered a traitor; she would have been taken away by the IRA's notorious internal security team for questioning. She would have been beaten to within an inch of her life and, if she was lucky, maybe dumped near her home with instructions to leave the country within twenty-four hours. The only reason she might just have escaped execution was because she was not a sworn-in member of the terrorist organisation. The Provisional IRA have a strict code of orders for their volunteers; one of these orders states that executions cannot be carried out on people who have not received the instructions contained with the Green Book. Donnelly, however, would have been fully conversant with the contents and was himself at risk for any information he passed on to Brenda that might have been deemed to be a threat to IRA operations.

One day Brenda told us that Donnelly was under the impression that he was the subject of some form of surveillance.

She told me that she nearly died on the spot when he came out with this statement. He believed that someone was investigating him and that for some reason he was likely to be picked up and arrested for questioning if he was not careful. She pressed him a little further on this but he was not forthcoming with any information – just that he was worried about them finding out things about him. She did the right thing and played the subject down – this only encouraged him to keep talking. He then told her that from time to time he received mail from a friend who lived abroad, and it was a possibility that it was because of this that he was under suspicion. Once again she lightly asked him how receiving mail from a friend abroad was likely to cause him problems. He didn't answer the question. Instead he asked Brenda if he could use her address for his mail. She agreed. He asked her if she could telephone him straight away when she received any mail for him, and he would appreciate it if she could bring it to him at his home on the evening that it arrived.

At this stage we were not aware of where the correspondence would be coming from. He was very clandestine about this. But he obviously trusted her and we would get to know in the end, so we all waited with eager anticipation.

Several weeks passed by and Brenda, along with Declan, each still unaware of the other's role, continued with the supply of information on the same target. Declan had made comments to the effect that he was keeping a low profile these days. He was not seen in the pub so often and one of the locals had told him that he had been seen with some bird with long legs and big tits – a good visual description of a standard we had come to expect from him.

Brenda rang me one morning; a letter had arrived for him. She said that I would definitely be stunned by the postmark and stamp; they were of great interest. She asked whether I could meet her now as he had already phoned and left a message on her answermachine, asking if anything had arrived; he knew the letter would be due. I quickly arranged for the team to be briefed before we deployed to the area of her pick-up. It was a fast-ball job and the orders were given in about ten minutes flat. They covered the salient points and that was about it — off we went.

As Mike drove past in the cover car he informed the rest of the team that Brenda was walking along her route as arranged. She would keep to the left-hand side of the road and proceed towards a shop about one mile away from her house — this was her cover story. I steadily approached the area of the pick up from the north, and as I approached her she gave me a signal that could only mean trouble. A split second later I pressed the microphone pressel and transmitted the message 'Abort, abort, abort'. I carried on driving straight past her and continued along the road away from the area. For Brenda to give me this signal meant there must have been something drastically wrong which I had not seen. It was the first time she had done this. What the hell was going on? I built up speed and headed back to base along with the remainder of the team. About twenty minutes later we arrived back at our detachment and I headed straight into the operations room. There had been no telephone calls from her. An hour slowly passed and then the telephone rang. It was Brenda. The duty operator handed me the telephone. Had I seen him? she questioned. Seen who? I asked. The object of our interest had turned up at her house to pick up the letter. She had seen me approaching and was just getting ready to jump into my car when she had glanced down the road to see a car similar in colour to one she had seen him use previously coming up the road. She had taken the right course of action and had called off the pick-up as she had been briefed. Just as well — it was him. The cheeky bastard had entered the area quite openly. He was obviously very keen to pick up his mail.

Brenda said that she could not really say any more on the telephone at that precise moment. I asked her why not, and she said that as she was talking to me she was watching him turn his car around in the driveway. He had been to the shop with her after she had aborted our operation. They had returned and had been to bed for a quick session – that was why it had taken her this long to get in touch with me. She had told him of one or two things she had forgotten to get at the shop and he had kindly volunteered to go and fetch them for her. He was now back. I told her to make a quick call to a friend after she put the receiver down on me so that if he was inquisitive enough to ask who she had been speaking to she would have a suitable answer to give him. Before she hung up she quickly told me that the letter had come from a country where a certain 'Mr Gaddafi' lived. Bingo.

Declan rang. He wanted to meet me as soon as possible – nothing too urgent, but it would not wait for our weekly meeting which was some four days away. A pick-up was arranged for the following morning. It was market day in the area, which provided a useful cover story for him to travel into our patch. He was, by now, following his orders perfectly, although we still had to implement all the standard anti-surveillance procedures to keep a check on him. Declan was the type of bloke who would go slightly off the rails should he feel that we had given him a little leeway. The pick-up ran very well; he had followed his route exactly as he had been briefed. Then came the 'Declan factor' – in the back of the car was a fully grown pig. I roared with laughter as he told me that he thought it was a good alibi for him being on our patch on market day. At least he was thinking along the right lines, even if they were slightly eccentric, but that was Declan.

He said he had some good information regarding our subject. Firstly it had been mentioned locally that our target had been arranging comprehensive training days for his 'volunteers'. He had apparently been spending a lot of time abroad, and the rumour was that he was receiving instructions in weapons and explosives in Libya. Declan, foolishly, had tried to follow the man in his car the day before. He then told us that he had been keeping out of the way of the authorities by going along the old country routes between the two main towns in the area, and had been seen heading east towards one of the old forestry tracks. Luckily Declan had lost him along the route, but was able to get to ascertain the general direction the man was heading in before losing sight of him.

Declan had obviously followed the man as he was on his way to visit Brenda. Without giving anything away I told Declan that his information was very useful. It corroborated other rumours we had heard. I told him to stop the following, just in case he was compromised. Declan told me that he had also followed him the day before, and said that the target, along with one or two other people, whom he named, had gone up to an area known as the Old Moor. He had made a note of their vehicle registrations. The men he had followed had gone quite a long way into the mountainous area, and Declan had heard shots being fired about half an hour later. The big picture was coming together. Our man was definitely the training officer for the Provisionals in that area. He was definitely getting outside training from the Libyans. What we needed was information on their weapons — when were they arriving, how were they transported, and how could we arrange an intercept. All this information had to be collected and the tasks accomplished without compromising our sources.

Brenda continued to keep us up to date on our target's actions and movements, virtually on a daily basis. Any little thing he said or mentioned was reported in detail. We had to get our hands on at least one of those letters one way or another. I briefed her that on the next occasion a letter was due I needed to be informed immediately. A detailed plan was put together with Brenda for the next mail arrival. An army COT was set up in the area of her house. The subject of their surveillance was a house some one hundred metres further up the road. They were given specific instructions that at any time during the operation they might be required to carry out another task for us, and had to be ready to move to a different location immediately. Brenda was told that she was to monitor her telephone answermachine and that she should not pick up the receiver until she had heard who was speaking at the other end. If it was our man, then she was not to answer him under any circumstances. As soon as he rang her, for whatever reason, she was to contact us straight away.

A few days passed and then Brenda rang. It was seven o'clock in the morning. He had called and left a message – could she ring him if any mail arrived that morning. We deployed our operations team to the area of her house and the COT team was briefed that covert soldiers in civilian vehicles and clothes would be operating in close proximity to their hidden location. They were not to challenge any suspicious activity they saw under any circumstances. They would be briefed on the radio as the task took place.

A message was passed over the radio from our operations room saying that Brenda had rung. The mail had arrived and there was something to pick up – same handwriting, same postmark. I parked my car up along a covered track and walked to the rear entrance of Brenda's house. She knew I would be arriving and opened the back door to let me in. There she was in a see-through negligee looking extremely sexy – and she knew it! She had even put on her make-up. She had the coal fire roaring away and she offered me a cup of coffee. If this had been a different place at a different time I might well have adopted an alternative line of chat. This, however, was dangerous. I told her that in about ten minutes' time she would be visited by an army patrol. She was to be abusive to them and tell them to get the fuck off her land and leave her alone. She was then told to telephone the man while the army patrol was in the area of her house, and to tell him that she had burned the letter just in case the army found it.

I placed the envelope in a plastic bag and left. She looked quite disappointed that I had to rush away − I think she was hoping for more than a mail pick-up. As I drove out of the area I informed our operations room that I had the package and that our team was returning to base. The COT was told to move to the area of three houses in the vicinity and carry out a search of the outbuildings to these houses, one of which was Brenda's. She now had a suitable alibi for destroying the letter and her neighbours could corroborate the fact that the army had carried out the search at that time, if he enquired. I handed the letter to my operations officer, who left for Headquarters Northern Ireland. Arrangements had to be made for the next mail delivery.

Brenda phoned Donnelly, who was naturally annoyed about what had happened. She pleaded her case and told him that she would not want to get him into trouble for any reason. Luckily he agreed with her actions and told her she had definitely done the right thing. She continued to meet him regularly and pass us more good information. She was never asked to be involved any further in his activities other than to act as courier for his mail. We encouraged her to try to spend more time in his home. She was likely to gain more useful information that way. She did as she was asked and stayed with him there more regularly.

Eventually it had to happen. She told us that he had asked her to marry him. This was now getting a little out of hand, as she rightly pointed out. She told him that she was not interested in marriage, and just enjoyed his company for the social life and the sex. He continued to encourage her to get married. She stopped her regular overnight stays at his house and made it quite plain to him that she enjoyed her independence and did not want that altered in any way. He accepted this grudgingly.

The first letter we had collected from her was apparently passed on to the spooks in London, and being their normal selves they told us very little about the contents, other than that it contained evidence of Donnelly's direct contact with an outside terrorist organisation and that it was useful in their research into the bigger picture of the international contacts that the IRA were making. They were obviously keen for more. We had to be careful that Brenda's position was not compromised, or we could quite easily end up in a situation with grave consequences for her. She was always aware of this and had accepted the realities of what she had been doing for us.

We briefed her to tell the man that she wanted to stop the mail being delivered directly to her house – it would be more secure to use post office boxes, as she had done with him initially. After the last fiasco with the army turning up, and if his mail was that important and sensitive, she would prefer to pick it up away from her home and not put herself in a position of risk. She stressed that she would still be happy to be used as his courier, but only if she could pick it up in her own time, when she felt comfortable doing so. That way she could deliver it safely. Her arguments seemed sensible. He agreed with her that it was the best option.

Another detailed plan was put together for the collection of the next mail delivery. Brenda was told to check her post office box regularly and telephone in when there was something ready for collection. She was to leave it there until I told her to collect it, and then I would take it from her straight away. It was a ploy we had used in another operation with some success, enabling us to delay the information being passed without too much attention being drawn to the agent for the late delivery. The mail was then to be transported from our detachment as quickly as possible and handed to the spooks. We arranged that they could have the mail as long as it was redelivered to us within twenty-four hours. This way we could return it to Brenda and she could deliver it to him without arousing too much suspicion. We could not risk delaying any longer than that. They agreed to our request and we waited for the next delivery.

The deliveries continued for several months, and the various agencies concerned passed very basic information back to us and asked us to encourage Brenda to continue her liaison with the target. At long last they confirmed that at least one piece of information contained in one of the letters had led them to an intercept of a quantity of 'merchandise' due to be placed in the hands of an ASU. This was excellent news for the detachment. It was the reason for us being there – to save lives using the information we had gathered. Unfortunately they would not inform us of any more details, but at least it was encouraging. Brenda was never told of any of her successes. She continued to work with us on this task and others for several years. The mail deliveries eventually dried up after about a year. Donnelly cut his contact with her after she persisted in refusing to marry him, but she continued to provide us with useful information.

About a year or so later I was due to leave the detachment. Another team had been linked up with Brenda and I had very little to do with her day-to-day tasking. She would sometimes spot me when I was providing cover for her meetings and would ask the lads how me and Lofty were getting on – he had left about three months previously but I think she missed us.

Some years later I happened to be in London and met up with one of the 'spook' contacts at a party. He had been involved with our mail-run operation, and was aware of my interest in the content of the 'merchandise' that had been successfully intercepted. Strictly off the record, he told me that at least one consignment contained a large amount of Semtex explosive and a variety of weapons and ammunition, mostly AK47 assault rifles along with a number of semi-automatic pistols. Brenda had undoubtedly saved numerous lives. Unfortunately she was never to know what she had achieved as she could never be informed of her accomplishments. It would be far too risky for her.

Chapter 10

The Quartermaster

One hundred and twenty Kalashnikov AK47 automatic assault rifles and eighteen thousand rounds of 7.62mm ammunition, enough weaponry to provide a medium-sized military force with the capability to mount full-scale terrorist attacks with deadly consequences. This staggering amount of lethal fire-power was to be taken from the Provisional IRA early in 1986 thanks to information obtained from a long-time established source working for the FRU. Frank Hegarty was a man ensconced within the ranks of the terrorist organisation with an unsurpassable pedigree. His role within the IRA's quartermaster's department gave him access to the intelligence the FRU needed to locate and control this deadly haul of weapons.

The massive cache of arms and ammunition was stored in three separate hides, buried in underground bunkers and then carefully camouflaged by the Provisional volunteers who had helped to offload and store the arms at different locations in southern Ireland. One stash was hidden away just outside the small village of Carrowreagh, north of Ballinasloe in County Roscommon, and the other two secreted not far from the seaside town of Sligo on the west coast of the country in County Leitrim. All the contents of the hides were fully operational, ready for use, and were also ready to be covertly distributed to the Provisional IRA ASUs throughout the Province, when required, for deployment in a variety of terrorist attacks.

The Russian-developed Kalashnikov weapons have always been a favourite with terrorist factions worldwide. They are reliable, with the impressive capability of firing six hundred rounds of ammunition a minute. With an estimated thirty-five million being produced worldwide, they were very easily obtainable with the right contacts within the terrorists' global network.

The weapons and rounds of ammunition that were hidden in southern Ireland were one of several similar shipments delivered over the years by sympathisers in Libya. Probably the two most well-known examples of these 'donations' that were intercepted as they were being shipped into the country were those found on the *Claudia* and the *Eksund*. The *Claudia*, a Cypriot-registered vessel *en route* to the south-east coast of Ireland around the area of Waterford, was found to be carrying a substantial cargo of 250 rifles and 240 small arms, along with a variety of anti-tank mines and explosives. The *Eksund*, which was intercepted in French waters, was carrying over 150 tons of rockets, rifles and other munitions, including a vast amount of the light and easily handled Semtex plastic explosive. These were the main shipments safely taken out of the terrorists, hands — who knows the total amount that has made it through to be used in attacks over the many years of the conflict? Colonel Gaddafi had made little or no secret of his admiration for the Provisional IRA, and had actively offered to assist them in obtaining similar shipments for future terrorist attacks. The IRA hierarchy were only too pleased to accept such offers, along with the instruction of its volunteers in the use of such weaponry, with Libya acting as host to such training.

It had been ascertained, through detailed intelligence-gathering by the unit, that a Londonderry man living in the republican stronghold of the Shantallow estate was a dedicated and passionate gambler. The man, known locally as 'Franko', had been closely connected with the Provisional IRA's quartermaster's department for a number of years, but he had either relinquished this contact for personal reasons or, as was rumoured, had been relieved of his position by the IRA because of their knowledge of his gambling addiction. He was, quite possibly, considered by the Provos' appointed army council to be a liability to their operations. Any person who gambled to the degree that Franko did was always likely to be open to clandestine approaches of financial enticement from both our unit and Special Branch, and the Provos were well aware of this. Whichever of these scenarios applied to him did not really matter to us. If recruited, he could still be of use for his detailed inside knowledge, even if it was historic information, and so a thorough investigation of his circumstances was initiated and eventually a recruitment plan was put together.

While out walking in the open countryside on the northern outskirts of Derry, Franko would quite often see a lone man off in the distance slowly moving away. Franko, who was a very amiable man, would hurry along and try to catch up with this man, who was always just a few hundred yards away, only to miss out on the chance of speaking to him by a minute or so as he watched the man getting into a car and driving away. What Franko never realised was that this whole scene was being orchestrated just for him. It was known that because of his friendly nature he would try to chat to strangers. A four-man surveillance team from the FRU was covering his every movement from the time he stepped out of his house, walked up the street and began one of his daily walks. The team would relay detailed messages by radio to the operative, stating exactly what Franko's location was, and how near to him he had progressed. This way the operator was able to stay a reasonable distance away without having to turn and look to see where Franko was located. The complex 'cat and mouse' game would be played out most days for about twenty minutes to half an hour.

The man off in the distance taking his country walk would always be just that little too far away for Franko ever to make personal contact. The object of his interest would never look back in his direction, which meant that Franko was unable to attract his attention. It was to become an earnest labour of love for Franko. He just somehow had to meet this man.

After a period lasting some weeks, the detachment boss, in consultation with his operators, had decided that it was about time that personal contact was made. There had been enough dangling of the carrot. Franko was probably wound up enough for a successful first-time meeting with the man, who for so long had somehow managed to evade him. The surveillance team were deployed and staked out Franko's house. After about an hour he was seen walking along his usual route and the operator was informed of his location by the team covering his every move. Out along one of the country paths to the west of the city, the operator slowed down his walking pace. Franko seized the chance to increase his and finally caught up with his quarry. They had met at last. The rapport was virtually instantaneous. Further meetings and walks with the man were arranged, and Franko and his new-found friend were often observed together, shadowed by a full covert surveillance team. Eventually the operator told him exactly what he was and the question of working as an informant was put to Franko. After several lengthy discussions of his potential role, he was successfully recruited to work as a paid source for the unit. At one covert meeting, quite some time after he had been recruited, Franko made the comment that he had been expecting an approach like this to be made to him for several years. He was totally amazed that it had taken this long for it to happen.

Frank Hegarty was in his early forties. He was a true Derry man, born and bred in the Rosemount area of the Bogside. He lived with his common-law wife and her children, and although he had not directly been involved actively with the Provisionals for a number of years, he still had his personal contacts within the organisation and the potential to return to their ranks should he be able to contain his gambling addiction. He had previously been listed by the unit's intelligence collators, who had gathered the detailed information on him, as a likely quartermaster within the provisional IRA, and it was to this particular branch of the Provisionals that he was actively encouraged to return. His handlers worked for many weeks to ensure a successful outcome. After many long discussions and briefings he eventually agreed to their requests – with certain reservations. He was offered a controlled amount of money to inform on the organisation on his return. Maybe the knowledge that he could obtain payments of cash in return for his information was the major factor in his recruitment, although one of his handlers, who had been one of my instructors, once told me that he was also motivated in a very much more idealistic way. He had genuinely grown to hate the violence that was wrecking his beloved home town and country.

During this particular period in Northern Ireland political tensions were much higher than had been seen for a number of years. Unionist politicians, as always, were up in arms over the progress being made in the Anglo-Irish agreements between London and Dublin, which they viewed as a betrayal. Their loyalist followers were all for breaking any acceptance of offers that came from Dublin, and once again loyalist paramilitaries took the lead in demonstrating their outrage. Violence erupted at many Apprentice Boys parades throughout the country, only this time the RUC, long seen as a traditionally Loyalist ally, was to take the brunt of the many attacks that followed. Several RUC police officers and their immediate families were to find themselves under real threat of violence from within their own communities. In the region of about fifty of their homes were petrol-bombed and burnt out. Along with a greater number of ordinary Catholic households facing the same kind of ferocious hatred in retribution for other attacks, it was a violent tit-for-tat situation that had not been seen in the Province for several years.

Over a few months Franko made it clear to the Provisional army council that he was available for full-time active service again. He rejoined the Provisional IRA ranks with no problems. He was welcomed with open arms by the army council and was sworn back into the organisation according to the rules laid down in the Green Book. He then managed to return to his old role within the quartermaster's department. He would again be responsible to the army council for the storage, allocation and deployment of all their weaponry. The role was suitable both to Franko himself and his handlers – they were obviously keen to re-establish him in this section of the IRA. It was an ideal situation.

Within the quartermaster's section he would not be required to carry out any hands-on terrorist actions. He had in any case become totally disenchanted by the whole situation of the Troubles and was not the type of man who would directly want to carry out bombing or shooting operations himself.

He would, however, have in-depth information on all major arms and ammunition caches, along with details of where they were hidden and when they would be required for use. The FRU now had a source in an ideal position to provide top-class pre-emptive intelligence that would save many lives in the Province over the coming years.

At this particular time the governments in both London and Dublin were locked in delicate discussions over the implementation of the agreements contained in the Anglo-Irish accord, which had been signed by both the Prime Minister, Margaret Thatcher, and the Irish Taoiseach, Dr Garrett Fitzgerald, in November 1985. This paper was to become known as the Hillsborough Agreement. The accord's aims were to find an agreement between the two countries as to how lasting peace and stability could be returned to the Province, while recognising the rights and wishes of both communities – a nightmare scenario. For both Thatcher and Fitzgerald there was a real urgency to provide the foundation for this accord to work. Give and take was definitely required from both sides. London did have something to give Dublin. Franko had detailed knowledge of some of the largest arms and ammunition caches in southern Ireland. This was the perfect opportunity to demonstrate that Downing Street was prepared to let the Irish Taoiseach be the recipient of a major intelligence coup, and it would also be a significant public relations bonus for both governments to show that they were prepared to work together on all angles of the Hillsborough Agreement.

The details of these weapons hides and their deadly contents were to be handed over to the southern Irish authorities sooner rather than later. The weapons were recovered by the Gardai and the Irish Army. Someone would have to suffer for this. Franko would become the fall-guy and he would have to be removed. No doubt this would present a minor irritation at governmental level. At detachment level it was a catastrophe. A contingency plan had to be put in place immediately.

Franko received a knock on his front door late that evening at his Shantallow estate home as he watched television with his common-law wife and her five children. The men at his door were his two agent-handlers from the FRU. He looked at them quite calmly and straight away asked them if it was time to go. He had had a feeling that something like this was going to happen. They nodded. Franko swiftly closed the door behind him and walked off with the two men to their car, not even pausing for a second glance behind. He had not even said goodbye to his family – he probably thought there would be too much to explain and not enough time to do it in. He was about to leave Londonderry for the first time. His return would not be an easy matter.

Franko was brought to England that night by his two handlers and was quickly relocated to a village close to the north coast of Kent. His family were totally unaware of his double life. The role of the informant is an isolated and dangerous one, where even the closest household members are never privy to their loved one's clandestine activities.

The unit handlers were to stay with him for several weeks under the guidance of another covert unit based in southern England. This specialist unit was specifically set up by the intelligence community. Run by experienced ex-handlers from our unit, it carried out the administration of relocated sources, looking after their initial requirements right through until the day they were allowed to be alone again, to try to run their own lives independently. It was a completely secret organisation in the true sense of the word. I knew a few of the operators in the unit personally, but their role remained that of an undercover operation – the people they were dealing with were on other people's death lists. Franko was to be debriefed by a number of other agencies and organisations as well as ours. He had lots of information stored away in his memory that would be extremely useful. Eventually, basic responsibility for his day-to-day activities was handed over to one of these other agencies. At the end of this extensive period he was left very much to his own devices. He had been allowed visits from his common-law wife, who had been completely shocked by the revelation of his situation.

Apart from being monitored on a casual basis by his new team, which had by now taken over the baby-sitting role from our operators, he was allowed to enjoy a fairly flexible lifestyle. This flexibility and freedom were to be his ultimate downfall.

The people of Northern Ireland have what can only be termed as a 'homing pigeon' instinct. Franko, like many others, displayed this syndrome. He just had to get home to his beloved Londonderry. He had become extremely homesick. It is also widely believed that he had come increasingly to regret his betrayal of his fellow countrymen when he had thought deeply on what he had done while working for our organisation. He had struck a phenomenal blow to their armed struggle by imparting the information on the caches. However, it is thought he believed that he could return to Londonderry and explain his actions to the army council and be allowed to settle back into the fold, if only he was allowed to contact someone in a position to protect him. At this time the Provisional IRA hierarchy was carrying out an internal investigation into the circumstances in which the arms and ammunition were discovered. They were in turmoil and desperate to find the source of the betrayal. A number of their volunteers had inside information on the exact locations of their weaponry and were all interrogated, but Franko was the only one to have disappeared, just prior to the find. No one knew where he had disappeared to. His guilt was confirmed by his actions.

Franko was living in a relaxed style, well catered for by the organisation in the village in Kent. His team of bodyguards and minders was loosely monitoring both his movements and his telephone calls. He made several calls home to the Province, mostly to his common-law wife. One of these calls is believed to have been made to an old friend and contact of many years, Martin McGuinness. McGuinness, it is rumoured, encouraged Franko to return home, saying he would ensure his safety. He was probably the only man in the Province who could make such an offer, one that Franko could truly believe in. There was to be no retaliation. He was told that the republican community sympathised with his position and realised that he was under some form of pressure from the Special Branch. He should have followed the example of Raymond Gilmour, another Provisional member of the IRA and a Special Branch source who had been compromised. He too had made various calls home whilst in hiding and had received the same sort of promises during a telephone conversation with McGuinness. He very shrewdly ignored the assurance of complete safety if he were to return to the Province.

A body was spotted trussed and taped up by a Gardai patrol, close to the border near Castlederg in County Tyrone. They informed the RUC of the presence of what looked like a corpse in the area. Frank Hegarty had been summarily executed with a single bullet in the back of his head, and had undoubtedly been tortured whilst under interrogation prior to his demise. His murder has been the subject of many lengthy inquiries and in-depth investigations, not least by the research team from the television programme *The Cook Report*. From information painstakingly gathered over the years they believed that McGuinness was directly involved, along with others, in giving the order for Frank Hegarty to be executed. Roger Cook and his team actually went to the extent of 'doorstepping' McGuinness at his home in the Bogside, asking him to talk about his role in the events leading up to Franko's death. Seamus Mallon, the SDLP leader at the time, described Hegarty's murder as an example of the Provisionals' own shoot-to-kill policy. McGuinness in turn threw the blame directly on to Special Branch and British Intelligence, stating that if these agencies did not force people into becoming informers they would never have to face the consequences of their actions. No one has ever been charged with his murder.

Franko had been well and truly 'conned' into thinking he could return safely to a life in his beloved Northern Ireland. He had given his minders in Kent the slip and had somehow managed to return unnoticed. He would surely have known the risks involved. General Order number eleven in the IRA's Green Book states that 'Any volunteer who seizes or is party to the seizure of arms, ammunition or explosives which are being held under Army control, shall be deemed guilty of treachery. A duly constituted court-martial shall try all cases. Penalty for breach of this order: Death. As in all other cases of death penalty, sentence must be ratified by the Army council.'

The explosives contained in that cache would have caused untold damage to property and loss of life in both the Province and on the mainland. The staggering number of weapons would likewise have been used in killings in both territories. Frank Hegarty undoubtedly saved numerous lives by passing his information. He paid the highest price for having done so.

Chapter 11

Shall I, Shan't I?

I had been sitting around at the detachment office one quiet Monday morning, my legs stretched out on my desk, avidly reading a new *Rugby World* magazine and drinking a cup of coffee while pretending to catch up with reading some important but well out-of-date paperwork marked for my attention, when one of the intelligence cell corporals from the local regiment at Lisnaskea rang me up. He asked if I was likely to be calling in for a chat at their office at some stage that week. Lisnaskea is a medium-sized market town situated on the eastern side of Upper Lough Erne, which is geographically a few miles to the south of Enniskillen.

Being in a completely idle mood and heavily engrossed in a paragraph in the magazine about the potential return of Welsh international rugby to the golden years of my teenage days, I was about to ask how important he considered the visit to be and, if it wasn't too crucial that I saw him that day, make a pathetic excuse to delay the visit to the following day. Just then the office door sprang open and the boss walked in. He looked over to me speaking on the telephone, interrupted my conversation and asked if I was doing anything very important later that morning. Anticipating something more likely to tax my grey matter than the first request from the corporal at Lisnaskea, I instantly jumped up and stated that yes, I was up to my eyes in paperwork and on top of this I had been summoned to Lisnaskea on an extremely hot tip-off. The boss looked at me, gave me a wry grin, shook his head and said that he thought I was a waffling bastard. He grinned again and walked off back to his office muttering something about no one having any respect for the chain of command and the Queen's commission; quite correct.

On the surface Lisnaskea seemed subdued. However, it was not exactly the cleverest place I had been to, and driving down the main street could be testing. People would stare at you, and on occasions I had got the feeling that they were looking at me with some knowledge of what I was, and what I was doing there. I could feel their eyes burning into the back of my head as my car was held up in a queue of traffic behind a slow-moving cattle truck or by a farmer trying to get his sheep up the High Street to the market. Nowhere else had this effect on me, just Lisnaskea.

Because of my personal opinion of the place I had always made a point of taking my support weapon with me every time I went there. This was my Heckler and Koch HK53 machinegun, a weapon with a fully sliding butt that was easily jammed in between my driver's seat and the door. I never intended getting out of the car on my way through the town, but if I had to at any stage it would be coming with me, and there would be a lot of noise and muzzle flashes coming along as well. I had read a report from one of the surveillance operators at the group who had been involved in a fatal 'contact' with some armed men in the Creggan Heights area of Londonderry a number of years previously. He had killed the terrorists outright with exactly the same type of weapon. His only comment was that 'on automatic, a full magazine on a "53" doesn't last long, but it does its job'. That was good enough for me.

On my various and frequent trips to this part of the world my other little habit was to take along an extra 9mm Browning pistol. This personal weapon would be placed under my left thigh facing the rear of the car. Both these weapons were obviously completely out of sight, but could easily be brought into use if the situation demanded. In the event that I was stopped by some unsavoury characters the pistol would be used to dispatch anyone who approached me without having to go through the rigmarole of drawing it from a waistband holster. A split second gaining the upper hand in the draw could mean a whole world of difference in a life-or-death situation. Illegal vehicle checkpoints mounted by the Provisional IRA in the border areas were a realistic threat. They had been carried out before in broad daylight at Carrickmore in County Tyrone, when they had wanted to make a show in what they considered to be their dominated areas. This was not purely an exercise in overreaction on my part; it was plain common sense.

I arrived at the barracks in Lisnaskea about half an hour later and drove through the barriers into the main carpark. After parking my car I hid my support weapons and walked down to the unit intelligence cell and asked to speak to the collator who covered the south-eastern patch of the area. He was an extremely switched-on Scots Guardsman who was very enthusiastic about his intelligence collation work. These intelligence cell soldiers are given a briefing at the beginning of their tours on the requirements of the FRU, and the basic techniques employed by the unit to target informants. They are encouraged to inform the FRU when any personalities are brought to their attention whom they think may be of interest to the unit.

This man's area of interest was the border region, which encompassed the whole of the Lisnaskea area right through to

Clones, a market town to the west of Monaghan that harboured some very hardline Provisional terrorists as well as being famous as the home town of Barry McGuigan, rechristened the 'Clones Cyclone' after becoming a household name through his boxing prowess.

Situated midway on the road between Newtonbutler and Clones is an army vehicle checkpoint. The soldiers who control it monitor all the traffic and the odd pedestrian coming through from Eire into the North. Details of every vehicle are logged as it passes through and returns. These details are stored on a master computer and are a good source of information for tracking the movements of people and vehicles. This particular corporal had been doing his job properly. He had found out from the Military Police roadman at the checkpoint that a man who had recently been released from the Maze prison was crossing the border on a regular fortnightly visit. He lived in a small village some miles away and his crossings formed a definite pattern. Research by the corporal had shown that he had apparently been imprisoned some fifteen years previously for terrorist offences related to the carrying of explosives.

He was also reported to have been a very close friend of both Seamus Maclewaine and James Lynagh, two notorious Provisional terrorists in their time, both of whom had met with violent deaths carrying out their terrorist activities. They were both killed by members of the SAS. Seamus Maclewaine had been at the electronic firing device end of a command wire attached to a large amount of explosive hidden under a culvert, not far from a combined police and army outpost, with the intention of exploding the device as the military or police vehicles went over it. Another Provisional named Noel Lynch was with Maclewaine at the firing point. When the SAS ambush opened fire on them he managed to extricate himself under cover of heavy mist. Maclewaine was killed instantly while

Lynch, even though injured, managed to roll down the hill, get into a ditch and crawl away. The QRF was crashed out to the area immediately. It is rumoured in certain circles that Lynch was found by the ambush team just after a Royal Army Medical Corps captain had arrived on the scene. The captain allegedly put a block on the operation being continued to a truly conclusive end, and Lynch ended up in the Maze prison, while Maclewaine was buried with all the trimmings of a true Provisional IRA martyr.

James or Jimmy Lynagh, on the other hand, was part of the IRA ASU that carried out the infamous attack on the RUC police station at Loughgall. He, along with Paddy Kelly and Padraig McKearney, two of his fellow Maze prison escapees, were caught in an ambush while in the process of getting out of a van to form part of the assault on the police station. They, along with Declan Arthurs, Eugene Kelly and Seamus Donnelly, were killed by the SAS operation, which left eight members of the Tyrone brigade of the Provisional IRA ASU dead. Both of these successful reactive operations had been enabled by pre-emptive intelligence information being correctly used in a timely manner.

The man on whom the intelligence cell corporal had built up the information was now of interest to me. He would be useful for both historic and pre-emptive information regarding his terrorist activities, particularly if I could get at him during the early days of his release. It had been ascertained that his regular fortnightly visits into the area were for the purpose of conducting a secret liasion with a married woman; once again a candidate for extra earnings from us in exchange for useful information. I had the ear of the Scots Guard NCO and told him that I was very grateful for his information but that I would probably want him to suspend his interest in the man he had been working on. He jokingly told me that he 'had already forgotten what I had said'.

I set to work formulating a plan to recruit the man, and took the Military Police corporal into my confidence. I asked him to report to me any pattern-of-life-forming characteristics this character displayed when he came through. There were none at the time. I grabbed a chance to try to meet him face to face. The first time I spoke to him he blanked me completely. He stared ahead and barely said anything at all, just muttering a few swear words in a quiet Southern accent which was barely audible. I asked him about his time in the Maze prison. He just looked at me and stated that I had all the records; why didn't I read about it?

He was going to be very hard work. After all, these people are briefed that when they leave prison they are likely to be the subject of an approach by agencies such as ours. They are told to report any such approaches to their own internal security teams and are well briefed on the way they are to handle any bribes, blackmail attempts or similar advances that may induce them to pass information. The terrorists' own internal security officers are a formidable force to be reckoned with. They were known to conduct intensive inquiries on possible informers. These would sometimes lead to interrogations being carried out on these suspects, with the death penalty being dealt out if it was proved that the guilty party had passed information – the ultimate deterrent.

I set about trying to befriend the man and generally become an acceptable face to whom he might talk. After about three months of my working hard on him he started to have very 'guarded' conversations with me about his past, but was never forthcoming on anything of any particular use to our detachment. I was on the verge of concluding the operation, either by coming straight out with the fact that I could pay him substantial amounts of money for any useful information he could give me, or by just knocking it on the head completely and letting him crack on with his life. I discussed the options with the boss and he suggested that I stick with it and continue to try to build up the rapport.

On the way back to our detachment after such a chat with him, I decided to nip into Lisnaskea and have a meeting with the intelligence cell corporal about someone else in his area in whom I was interested and cadge a decent cup of coffee.

I had been in the cell for about a quarter of an hour when a young captain from the Scots Guards walked in. He was the Intelligence Officer for the unit and introduced himself as such. We shook hands. He asked me if I wouldn't mind having a chat with him in private in his office after I had finished in the main intelligence cell. I told him that I would be more than happy to and would be along in a few minutes' time. I thought there was something a bit iffy about the situation when he looked at me and said in his best Eton, Sandhurst and Guards accent, 'Well, I think you're just about finished in here now, don't you?' I let him go on his way and finished my coffee. The corporal I was chatting to made a motion with his clenched fist and muttered the word 'wanker' under his breath. I laughed at this comment, then ambled down the corridor to the captain's office.

I knocked on his door and he called out for me to enter. He looked at me over his desk as I stood in front of him and said, once again in his acquired accent, 'Sergeant, when I infer I require your presence in my office, that is exactly what I mean. Do you understand, Sergeant?' I thought to myself, fucking hell, I've got a right one here, and so I explained that I had unfinished business with the staff in the intelligence cell. He interrupted me in mid-sentence. 'I take it you mean my staff, in my intelligence cell.' I thought, Back off, Rob, you're on to a loser here. The way he was making a point of stressing the rank thing was obviously some sort of power trip. He was marking his turf, and it was obvious that he expected me to be as subservient to his demeanour as one of his guardsmen. We started to have a conversation, or should I say he had a conversation – I was the audience.

He went on to tell me that he had developed a 'theory' of intelligence he was hoping to have named after him eventually, rather like the 'Winthrop' theory, by virtue of which search teams over the years had been encouraged to look at obvious physical points on the ground in order to locate weapons hides and caches. A certain Royal Engineers officer named Winthrop had noticed that the majority of significant arms finds in the Province occurred at points that could easily be described to another person, such as near a large oak tree by an electricity pylon on a main road, the oak tree being the only one around. Mr Winthrop had this notion that should a third party be sent out to pick up the contents of a hide they would have to have definite leaders to be guided to the exact point.

After a period of time the Provisionals cottoned on to this as well, and it ceased to work after a few years. However, fair play to the bloke, it turned up some extremely good search results for quite a while. The Winthrop theory was well known throughout the army.

My little Jock 'Rupert' had one mission in life – to get a similar 'theory' named after himself. I felt like telling him that 'tosser' was already in the dictionary and was hardly a theory, and there were plenty of other theories about without him having one all to himself to enthral pretty young things in Chelsea at dinner parties. Nonetheless I was vaguely intrigued, and I was going to hear it anyway, whether I liked it or not. His theory was that the various intelligence agencies were not talking to each other. I thought, Please, tell me something I don't know. He continued that if a system could be formulated wherein all these agencies pooled their resources and their knowledge, and let a single entity deal with all the information to disseminate as they saw fit, then everybody would have access to any worthwhile intelligence that could be of assistance to them. We would be much more aware of the big picture and get more results. He would formulate and run the show personally and we could call it 'the Macsomething or other theory'. The basics of it all were sound enough, but having lived in this murky world I knew that he was completely out of his depth — the powers that be would not even have him near their office doors, let alone allow him to run their intelligence collation systems. He was dreaming if he thought otherwise.

After he had tied my brain cells up in knots over his little 'theory', I said, 'You would probably be better off putting it on paper and letting Headquarters Northern Ireland have your thoughts.' I started to make my excuses to get away from this nutter, and said that I would probably pop in early the following week to have a chat with 'his' intelligence cell personnel. They were quite a good bunch of lads and very helpful, so I told him as much. It does not do any harm, but I really think this bloke was so wrapped up in himself that he would not have given a monkey's about anyone else anyway. As I was leaving his office he shouted, 'Don't forget to book out with your journey details.' I poked my head back around his door and said very politely that I did not really have to do that. He then told me that if I didn't put down my route in his operations room he would telephone the guardroom and order the gate guard to stop me from leaving the camp. I thought to myself, Oh, really, now this will be interesting. I knew I was definitely on to a winner the way this one was going — this snooty little fucker was about to become unstuck.

I went straight back into his office and told him that I worked for an independent unit and that we had no obligation, under any circumstances, to let anyone outside our own unit have details of any tasks we were involved in, or to divulge any travel movements. We were completely unrestricted in this. He looked at me with complete amazement and told me that I would have to get authority from Brigade Headquarters, so I said, once again in a very polite manor, 'Fuck Brigade, sir, phone the chief of staff at Headquarters Northern Ireland.' He looked at me and held his hand over the phone while he asked me who he should say was claiming authorisation to travel unrecorded and unaccounted for by his intelligence cell. I said to tell the chief of staff that it was 'Rob from West Detachment'. The man looked at me vaguely and said, 'Who?' Again I said, 'Tell him it's Rob from West Det. It's OK, he knows me; in fact, after you've finished chatting to him I'll have a quick natter. He's supposed to be coming down fishing at the weekend.' He looked at me as if I were a Martian. I'm not sure if he thought I was bluffing or not. He was not about to put it to the test, but I was wishing he would. It was quite true.

He then stated that he was not about to phone the chief of staff over something so trivial, so why didn't I just be a good man, book out and be about my business. I thought to myself, No way, you arrogant wanker. I stood my ground and refused point blank to agree with his demands. After a few minutes I had just about had enough of this jobsworth and so I said, once again very politely, that I was about to phone my commanding officer and he could deal with him direct. I asked to use his phone and dialled the CO's direct line. The commanding officer at the time was a cracking bloke who had been the main instigator of our unit gaining its independent status. He answered and I said 'Hi, Boss, it's Rob here from West.' The Jock Rupert's face was one of pure disgust at the thought of me calling my CO 'Boss'. I explained the situation and the CO simply said, 'Put him on, Rob.' I passed the phone over and for the next ten minutes a red-faced Rupert sat there repeating 'Yes, Colonel', 'No, Colonel' and nothing else. He then handed the phone back to me. The CO said that he did not think I would have any more problems with this guy. If there were I was to ring him straight away. Captain 'Macwhateverhisnamewas' then cleared his throat and said that there was no problem about my leaving 'his' camp and that I did not have to book out, but I should consider his position. No problem. He did not have a position as far as I was concerned. I headed back to our detachment.

I received a phone call from the Military Police corporal to tell me that the man from Clones in whom I had shown an interest had been through that morning. He had apparently told the roadman that he was off to the market in Lisnaskea. He said he could not really say anything at the moment, but asked if I was going to be going there at all that day. I told him I would travel down if he wanted to chat about something. He then told me it might be worthwhile – there had been an interesting development. There was third-party interest in the man.

We had another detachment of our unit not too far away, whose area of responsibility just crossed over with ours at the point where the checkpoint was situated, so I rang them. Dave, the Intelligence Corps bloke who had been on my course, answered, and we spent the next few minutes throwing various forms of abuse at each other, like how the fuck could I manage to get around without a Chieftain tank, and how it must be great for me being Welsh with all those sheep around, etc., etc. He got a fair amount of verbal slagging back, and he was taken a back a bit when I told him that I had heard that the Intelligence Corps motto was being changed to 'A pat on the back is only a recce' – a reference to the constant back-stabbing exploits of certain members of his corps who would do literally anything for faster promotion or to get better onward postings than their contemporaries. Jokingly he told me to stop being a bitch. After we had finished the banter I asked him about the man I was interested in and enquired if his detachment was digging into the same character. He emphatically stated that they were not interested and did not have any of their blokes in that area. No problem, I'd find out what it was all about. More abuse; end of call.

When I arrived at the area the roadman recognised me and pulled me into the roadside. We proceeded to have a chat while he went about 'pretending' to search the boot of my car. He told me that two blokes from Special Branch in Enniskillen had been down. They had asked about this guy in particular, and had spoken to him when he returned from market. Bastards — they never missed a trick. They even asked the corporal if I had been down chatting to him — not someone from my unit, but me personally. I headed back to the detachment and briefed the boss. He simply said, 'Don't fuck about, Rob; get in there and ask him the question,' referring to the fact that I had spoken to him often enough to pose the question now. If the man was open to the suggestion that he should work for a large and powerful organisation and earn lots of money for passing information, then I should make it. Our next move would be on Thursday.

Thursday arrived and I headed to the area where I knew I would come across the man. I hung around for about two hours, but my subject did not appear. He had a pattern of travelling in that area whereby he was normally seen at around ten o'clock. This day of all days there was no sign, so I packed up and sat in my car waiting for the 'all clear' from the roadman to drive out on to the highway. As I jumped in my car I wedged my Heckler and Koch down the side of my seat and placed the spare pistol under my thigh. On a quick signal I was out and away heading north towards Newtownbutler, a village just a few miles up the road. As I headed up the A34 I glanced in my rear-view mirror. Behind me I saw a familiar pale blue Vauxhall Cavalier; fuck me, it was him! He was about one hundred metres back and gradually getting nearer. I had an outrageous idea. In a split second I decided that I would let him overtake me. As he was parallel with me I would ram this fucker off the road, ditch my own car, run across and shoot him. Shall I, shan't I? Yes, come on, you fucker, overtake me, I said to myself. I had a convicted terrorist in the vehicle behind, and he knew me. It was plausible for him to try to kill me, a perfect scenario. I'd probably get a medal for this shit! Fucking hell, come on, overtake me!

I then had to slam my foot hard on the brake. In front of me was a police foot patrol carrying out a vehicle check. One policeman was in the road waving me down and directing me to another policeman about twenty yards away. As I drove into the checkpoint I noticed two policemen off to one side. It was the pair of blokes from Special Branch, in uniform, looking very sheepishly at me. They knew I recognised them; what a pair of twats. After passing through the check I headed straight to the detachment and mentioned my little shooting idea to nobody. I informed the boss about the Branch guys being at the check- point and the fact that the subject was the next car behind. Oh well, I thought, there was always a week Thursday. But there wasn't.

An article appeared in *An Phoblacht* and a few other papers the following week saying that a former member of the Provisional IRA had been given twenty-four hours' notice to move out of the Province. After such time, if he was still in the area, the security team from the Monaghan brigade of the IRA could no longer ensure his personal safety. Even though nothing had been proven it was suspected that he was passing information to the Crown Force occupiers in the Six Counties. Basically the bloke had to leave or he would be dead before the day was over. The article continued by saying that the young man mentioned had recently been released from the Maze prison and had been reported as being under constant abusive harassment from the RUC. With a little co-operation instead of obstruction, both ourselves and the police could have benefited from an extremely well-placed source. The man disappeared off the scene and was never sighted again during my time at the detachment.

Chapter 12

Breaking the Rules

Throughout the earlier part of my army career I had always been considered, and probably quite rightly so, as being a somewhat troublesome young soldier. After joining as a junior entrant at just over sixteen and a half years old, I had acquired the uncanny knack of dropping myself well and truly in the shit on a fairly regular basis through a variety of misdemeanours, which over the years were scrupulously recorded on my military conduct sheet. The conduct sheet records every occasion when I was required to be marched in front of an officer commanding the particular squadron I was with at the time, or, if the offence had been particularly serious, the times I was charged by the commanding officer of the regiment.

The offending conduct sheet entries were mostly classified under what Queen's Regulations quote as being covered by 'Section 69a of the Army Act 1955', and are worded 'in that he . . .', followed by the details of the particular offence committed – anything and everything that can be done to bring your particular unit or the army as a whole into disrepute. I had often mused about having this quote engraved on my headstone followed by the charge that I had died without gaining permission from the appropriate officer in charge.

My own particular conduct sheet made for some quite amusing reading (to me anyway), covering all sorts of crimes and misdemeanours I had been involved in over the years, including the theft of wines and spirits from the officers' mess, returning late from a leave period, being caught in an 'out of bounds' public house, fighting in a nightclub, using threatening behaviour in a public place and failing to attend a duty. Over the years it had cost me a lot of money in several hefty fines. Apparently these are all donated to the Army Benevolent Fund, in which case maybe I could apply to get them back in my retirement years!

The strange thing about this lengthy list of offences was that during my career they never really affected my promotion, and I was still on par with the majority of my contemporaries. In fact, after being reduced in rank to trooper I was subsequently repromoted rapidly, and overtook some of my mates who had not been promoted in the interim period, much to my amusement and no doubt much to their annoyance.

On initially applying for selection to the Special Duties course it had occurred to me that my damning conduct sheet might be my downfall. I had even gone to the extent of sneaking into the regimental headquarters one night to have a chat with the duty clerk with the idea of getting at my personal records under some pretext or other, and then lifting my conduct sheet out of them for personal disposal. Unfortunately for me they had already been packed, sealed and stamped by the chief clerk ready for me to take to the initial interview, and no amount of begging, sweet-talking or threats of physical violence could get the clerk to unpack them, let me have access to the contents, and then return them for him to reseal.

The following day, at the end of an exhaustive initial interview, I was questioned in some depth about my personal life. It was all part of the selection process, and at a crucial stage one of the panel pulled out my regimental conduct sheet. I winced. The interviewer then looked hard at me and asked whether I had ever been in trouble either in the services or in civilian life. I jokingly asked him if we were pushed for time, adding that I could come back another day, and as he looked down at the paper in front of him he gave me what can only be described as a wry grin. In my teenage years I had managed to get myself into a lot of trouble, and he was reading the details of my misspent youth. His co-interviewer, who was playing the nasty character in the scenario, told me not to try to be a comedian and just to answer the question, and so taking a deep breath I reeled off half a dozen of the offences I could remember being on the sheet. He then reminded me of the other four I had not mentioned. I nodded and agreed that they had slipped my mind. After a quick, private conversation with his companion, he said, 'Well done today, you put a lot of effort in. We think you are a suitable candidate for the selection to Special Duties.' I was given my instructions for the next phase and told to leave the building by the side entrance and to go straight to my car and drive out of the establishment without having any communication with the other prospective candidates. Bit of a hard one that, as two of the other candidates had got a lift with me from my own unit. I sneaked around the corner, spotted them in the corridor and whispered that I would see them in the café down the road. I would be sneaking around corners for a few years to come!

Breaking the rules would a few years later become a normal occurrence for me, particularly when it concerned my wayward social life outside of my working environment. I was never again to be charged for any offences by the army, but I certainly had a few mild bollockings for being out of order, whether intentionally or not. On one occasion an old friend of mine, who was on the resident SAS troop in the Province, rang me at our detachment to tell me about another mate of ours who was soon to be leaving Northern Ireland for Cyprus; he was having a departure piss-up in Belfast and was I interested in going up for the night? After making the arrangements for my accommodation at their place for the night I booked out of the detachment with our duty operator and headed up the motorway at speed.

On arrival at the Belfast detachment of 14 Intelligence Company (or 'the Group' as it was known to me then), I immediately met up with half a dozen of the blokes who were already in the bar. I knew most of them well from my previous time with the Group, and a few of the faces in the bar had been on the same course as me. Most of them I had not seen for a good while. It looked like it was going to be a good night. One of the lads involved in organising the piss-up had arranged for their duty driver to take us in a shuttle service over to the Stormont Hotel, and so after a few quick beers to warm up in their bar, we headed out across town to the hotel. This was quite a smart set-up which ran a nightclub cum disco and band night on certain evenings and whose customer base was essentially loyalist, and which was therefore cleared for us to socialise in. It was the only place I had ever been into socially in the Province where at the end of the night the band struck up the National Anthem. It is most amusing to watch a packed hall of pissed-up people trying to stand up and show their allegiance to the Queen. Those who were incapable of standing under their own steam were precariously lifted and held up by their friends until the band had finished.

During the early part of the evening I had been talking to an extremely attractive blonde-haired girl in her twenties at the packed-out bar. I had managed to convince her, or so I thought, that I was in the Province working for Short's in Belfast harbour, as a junior technical adviser at their electronics department. This was my alibi for being a 'Brit' on a quick visit to Northern Ireland for the weekend. I was based at the company's main electronics plant in the north of England. Don't ask me if there is one; I still don't know. It seemed to be credible to her anyway.

She proceeded to tell me that her name was Sarah, that she worked for the Department of Agriculture in the government buildings at Stormont, and that she was a civil servant of three years' standing who had been transferred from London to the Province on promotion; this explained her English accent. She said she was from Swindon originally. All this being accepted, she returned to her bunch of friends and I looked around for the gang I was with, having secured the chance of a further meeting with her later in the evening for a drink and a dance. It was far too early to go 'on the trap' – it would possibly cost a fortune in drinks. We used to have a saying in my regiment that you should 'go ugly early', meaning that you should chat up a not-too-attractive female, buy her drinks and sweet-talk her all evening in the hope of sexual activities later – she would probably be grateful for the offer. This girl, however, was far too good-looking, and I was not about to waste my hard-earned beer money on a possible lost cause.

I spent the next hour or so chatting at the bar about old times with one or two of the lads and generally swung the lantern about what we had been up to since we last met up. We gave our respective headquarters the usual slagging, along with Special Branch and the security services. This was all normal form for soldiers when they are out on the beer for the night, and particularly for the soldiers concerned in this particular conversation. The three of us were all from different covert units serving within the Province – Dean was in the SAS, Steve was from the Group, which specialised in covert surveillance, and I was from a source-handling unit. All three are regular

British Army units. All three are dedicated to the fight against terrorism, and all three are ruled by a hierarchy in the Province which likes to keep them well apart. There was a lot of paranoia on the part of other agencies with regard to the personnel of the units we served in being on speaking terms.

As the evening progressed it was decided that when the Stormont Hotel closed later, we would walk towards the main part of town, grab a pizza, take it back to the detachment bar and continue with an all-night piss-up.

I had been standing by the edge of the dance-floor for a few minutes, leching at the female talent on display, when the girl I had been chatting to earlier walked up to me and quietly said that she had not realised I was 'on the troop'. This is the well-informed insider's way of saying in the SAS. I nearly choked on my beer and told her I did not have a clue what she meant. She looked at me with a knowing smile and asked me how I knew Dean. To this I responded quite pleasantly that I didn't know who she was talking about. She informed me that she had been watching me, and I had been leaning against the bar for the last hour or so talking to him. After bluffing my way out of that one by telling her that she must have mistaken me for someone else, I was simply told that I should ask my friend and that he would know. Know what?

I kept away from Dean for a while and then managed to catch his eye and point at the girl and mime 'do you know her?' He came over and we had a quick conversation about her. Yes, he did know her; her name was Lisa, and she worked as part of the administrative staff for Box 500. The girl was a junior spook who worked for the security services, MI5. Department of Agriculture seemed quite an appropriate cover somehow. On spotting Dean and me chatting she waved to us and Dean called her over and introduced us, using our real names this time. He did not mention which unit I was with and left us alone for a quick chat. We both had a laugh about the cover story bullshit we had gone through earlier. The hotel disco was about to finish, and she asked if I wanted to go on to a party at their shared accommodation. I spotted the lads from our party heading towards the door and thought about the consequences of my unit background being found out, so with a grin and a quick kiss on the cheek I told her that I could not stand women who lied on their first date, and off I went. She must have thought I was off my rocker to turn her invitation down. I probably was.

The night came to an end eventually, and we somehow managed to track down all the other members of our party and returned, with large pizzas in hand, to the detachment bar and launched into what was to turn out to be a seriously major piss-up. The following morning I begrudgingly dragged myself out of a comfortable warm bed, into the shower and then into the canteen for a seriously loaded cooked breakfast, along with a gallon of tea. What I didn't know was that some of the lads I had been with the night before had been called out earlier on a surveillance job on an address on the city outskirts, to cover a weapon that was due to be moved from its hide by a source. This weapon was to be handed to a gunman for a hit to be carried out on a part-time UDR soldier later on that week. The source had informed his handler of the move just in time, and the surveillance operation was a success in as much as the weapon was still under observation by members of the detachment.

I met the team as I was leaving to head back to the wilds of Fermanagh. They were coming back in after being replaced by a fresh bunch of operators. They had managed to get little sleep the previous night, and all had hangovers to nurse; my own luckily had subsided by then. We exchanged a torrent of friendly abusive banter, and I then headed back towards the dual carriageway and drove south on the M1 motorway. I had had a really good night with them. Little did I know at the time, but yes, I was in the shit again.

Monday morning arrived with its usual predictability and I strolled into the detachment operations room, whistling some tune merrily to myself. I unloaded my Browning pistol and asked Sammy, one of the collators, if there was anything going on of any interest. He asked me if I had seen the boss yet, as he had been asking for me. It was unusual for the boss to be in before me, and so I walked up the corridor and put my head around his office door, jokingly said 'Boo!' and asked him if he wanted to see me. He looked up from the paperwork on his desk, said he did and could I come in and shut the door behind me; no smiles and an interview without coffee.

He asked me where I had been over the past weekend, and so I told him quite truthfully that I had been up to Belfast on Friday night, and then had spent the rest of the weekend fishing in the local area. He then told me that the operations officer had rung and wanted to see me personally, and I was to jump in my car and drive up to Lisburn. I complained that it would take me most of the day to do this and that I had things to do in the detachment, and would it not be more sensible for me just to ring him and find out what he wanted. The boss informed me that it was to do with my social night out on Friday; certain people wanted to know exactly what I had been up to. Here we go again, I thought. I could not think for the life of me how the operations officer could have found out about that night. I was more than curious.

I arrived at Headquarters Northern Ireland about an hour and a half later. I made my way down the corridor and was met by the commanding officer of the unit, who jokingly said that he was surprised that anyone from our detachment should know their way to headquarters, and if I was lost I should get directions from someone. Well, at least I did not appear to be in the shit with him, which was useful.

I knocked on the operations officer's door and walked in, which was the usual routine for a unit not given to the rules and regulations of normal military procedures, only to be told quite sharply to get back out again. The man in charge was an Intelligence Corps major by the name of Johnny. Johnny was a smartly dressed, dapper little man who had been quite highly decorated for gallantry in his younger days. The unit Intelligence Officer, Mike, had been in the office with him when I had walked in. Mike was a cracking bloke whom I knew well, extremely well liked by everyone in the unit — we had played rugby together on many occasions. Johnny, however, had a tendency to look upon people of lower rank and standing within the organisation with a certain amount of disdain, or maybe it was just me.

Mike was standing by the door and was about to leave the office when there was a call of 'In'. As Mike passed me he looked at me, grinned, shrugged his shoulders and raised his eyebrows. I walked into Johnny's office. He simply looked at me and said, 'Sit.' If I had been in a cockier mood I might well have rolled over and asked for a biscuit. He then asked me where I had been on Friday night and whom I had been with. I told him straight forwardly where I had been and who my companions were. He then began to question me in some depth as to the content of the conversations that had taken place between us that night. I truthfully informed him that the conversations were mostly personal and social and that at no time were operational plans, tasks or any sensitive information regarding our individual units discussed during the course of the evening. It transpired that one of the lads who had been with us that night had been chatting to a Special Branch officer he knew who had enquired who I was, and had asked which unit I was with.

After he had been informed he had gone telling tales about me at his own department, and my headquarters had been instructed to find out from me what I had been up to. The conspiracy theories must have been flying fast and low down the police corridors of power.

Johnny then proceeded to inform me that I was to have no further contact whatsoever with these so-called associates of mine at the Intelligence and Security Group or the SAS Troop, and that I was to confine my social life to my own kind or have none at all. The problem, as I explained to him, was that Dean lived in the same cul-de-sac as me back on the mainland, and that I had been Steve's best man some months previously – we were old friends from before we joined the army. How did he expect me to get around these personal factors? Did the Branch dictate what I did at home as well? With a dismissive wave at the door he told me just to be careful about whom I consorted with. He obviously had no answer to give me. This was not to be my last chastisement from Johnny.

My social life in the Province was to give me one or two more surprises over the next few years. One particular incident was to accompany me right up to, and beyond, my departure from both Northern Ireland and the army. On a Friday evening I had been asked by one of the lads at the detachment whether I was going out to a certain nightclub in the area on that particular night, and if I was would it be OK for him to come along with me. He was one of our junior collators. At that particular time the boss had imposed a rule that support staff could only go out socialising if they were accompanied by one of the operators, because of a certain number of cock-ups they had made during the previous two weeks. This particular collator, Ryan, was without a doubt one of the best blokes we had, and I had no problems with his request. Another of the operators, Lofty, had said that he would also be going to this club, and as he and I were sharing a house at the time there would be no problem with Ryan staying overnight at our place, albeit on the settee in the living room, unless he was able to 'score' with one of the local females, in which case he was on his own and we would cover for him.

The club we had decided to go to was a few miles' drive from Enniskillen. Ryan jumped in my car, planning to meet Lofty there later. We parked up in the well-lit carpark across the road from the club. The clientèle at this place was fairly mixed, both Protestant and Catholic, and it was not unknown for the doormen to carry out body searches on people they did not know well. With this in mind I slipped my Browning automatic pistol out of the hip holster and pushed it down the front of my jeans; with a thick leather belt and a sweat-shirt over the top it was impossible to see. It is a well-known fact of life that blokes do not like to be seen groping other blokes' balls, and I had been the subject of searches at this particular place before. They were not very thorough at all. Problems tend to arise later on in the night if asked by a female for a slow dance, when the old Mae West cliché about is that a pistol in your pocket or are you just glad to see me becomes a realistic talking point. The night was going quite well – the place was packed out with people enjoying themselves and the three of us were having quite a good laugh. There were a number of people we knew, both from the security forces and civilians, and we were invited back to one or two parties after the club shut. These invites were from policemen and UDR men and their wives, girlfriends and some of their friends. As the night progressed I found myself leaning against the bar alone for a few minutes as I tried to get served. I was joined by a strange-looking character who looked at me and asked me how I was doing. I told him I was doing fine, and he immediately asked if I was English. I told him that I was. He then came out with the odd remark that he knew me and that my name was Mark. As he said this my memory banks went into overdrive as I tried to recall whether I had ever used this name before when attempting to recruit a potential source and strove to put this bloke's face into the picture. I could manage neither. He was a complete stranger to me.

I told him that he must be mistaken. He then said that I was wrong and that my name was Mark and that he did know me. This emphatic statement reminded me of something I had been told by one of the instructors on passing my selection to Special Duties a few years earlier. He thought I had an uncanny resemblance to a previous operator who had been at the detachment I was going to and who had left some years before my arrival, and that I should not be surprised if I was questioned on the likeness at some stage in the future. He said that we could easily be mistaken for twin brothers. His name was Mark Francis; this, however was the first time it had happened. This bloke became more and more insistent about the fact that I was Mark Francis, and he was most inquisitive about what I was doing back in Northern Ireland and asked whether I was still working 'down below'. He nodded in the general direction of our base, an obvious reference to the military location we worked from. Once again I told him that I was sorry but he was completely wrong, I was not Mark Francis, and I reiterated that I did not have the foggiest idea what he was talking about. Before he left he asked me again if I was sure I was not Mark Francis. This guy was starting to get on my nerves, and so with a certain amount of irritation I looked him straight in the face and asked him how he knew this guy Mark, and if he knew him that well had he not realised by now that I was not the man in question. He backed off slightly, realising that I had my hackles up. He informed me that he did not really know Mark Francis himself, but that his girlfriend had known him — she had spotted me at the bar and had asked this character to come over and find out on her behalf. I told him that I was sorry to disappoint them, but he could tell her she had got it wrong. I moved off to another part of the club and found Lofty and Ryan with their faces well and truly into two of the local young ladies – their timing was perfect as the place was due to shut in about an hour. I decided to leave them to it and chatted to a policeman I knew quite well.

At about midnight Lofty tracked me down and said that he was off to one of the parties we had been invited to and that Ryan was going along with him. I found out where they were going and told them I might follow on later. They departed with the two girls I had seen them with earlier, and so I decided to call it a night about half an hour later and left the club, crossing the street to the carpark across the road. I was about fifty yards away from the car when a female walked out in front of me about ten yards away, looked at me and said, 'Mark Francis.' At the same time, out of the corner of my eye, I caught sight of a man skulking about near a wall over in a dark part of the carpark. It was the bloke from the club. My heart missed a beat. Fucking hell, here we go! I told myself that all I needed to do was rip the front of my sweat-shirt up, grab the pistol grip, put a few rounds of ammunition into the female and then empty the rest of the magazine over in the direction of where the man was still hiding in the darkness. A split second later her facial expression showed me that she realised she had got it wrong. She looked embarrassed and apologised for the mistake. I asked her if she could tell her friend to come over out of the darkness as he was starting to be a bit of a worry to me sneaking about in the shadows. She called over to him and he joined us. I asked about her interest in Mark Francis, and she told me that she had been out with him a few years before and that he had just disappeared back to England. She knew vaguely what his job was about in the Province and said that it had been a genuine case of mistaken identity – the likeness was remarkable. With

223 •

that said and done, we all said goodbye. I quickly checked under my car for any unwanted packages and headed out of the carpark towards home.

On the following Monday morning I strolled into the detachment as per usual, whistling merrily as I invariably did to annoy everybody. I had a quick chat with one or two of the lads and decided to walk across to the intelligence cell to cadge a cup of coffee and get an update on any incidents or interesting sightings of known terrorists in our area that had been reported over the weekend; basically anything that might be of use to me. As I walked into the corridor one of the UDR guys beckoned me over to his desk and laid out a few of the local newspapers, one of which had a photograph of a female at one of the local events in town. He asked me with a big grin on his face if I recognised her, to which, being completely mystified, I replied that I had never seen her before in my life. He asked me to have a closer look and a longer think. Once again I told him that the face did not ring any bells with me, and why was he asking anyway. He simply replied, 'Carpark, Friday night.' After a bit of a joke about this I asked him how he knew about this little episode, and he proceeded to tell me that the girl in question was his girlfriend's sister and that the Mark Francis lookalike incident had come up in conversation on the Sunday afternoon. As soon as he had heard about it he had realised that it was me they were discussing.

The girl in the carpark, and this bloke's girlfriend, whom I had seen before on a number of occasions, were both good-looking females, and I jokingly asked if there were any other spare sisters knocking around doing nothing that week. He told me to leave it with him. On the Thursday following this conversation I had a call from him asking me if I fancied a blind date with one of his girlfriend's sisters, Lynda. We met up that evening. The rest, as they say, is history, and we married a few years later after I had left the army. If I had shot the girl in the carpark that night things would have turned out very differently.

Over the next few years my social life in the Province was to undergo occasional hiccoughs. I had been staying overnight at Lynda's house a number of times during the week. I would do this when the duty operator at the detachment was one of my more trustworthy mates. My usual routine at these times would be to book out on the board in the operations room that I was going into town, and then tell the duty operator that I was staying out at Lynda's and give him the phone number. Not usually a problem, this continued for many months.

I had been asked to help out as an instructor for a few weeks on one of the selection courses for the detachment being run back at the training establishment in England, and thought it would be quite a good laugh. It was payback time for the misery and heartache I had gone through during my own selection. It would be a pleasant change to be on the other side. It was indeed good fun, and after I had finished I flew back to Aldergrove from Heathrow ready for whatever lay ahead back in the Province. I was met at the airport arrivals area by Ryan, and we headed out to the carpark. We jumped in the old van used for administration runs and I asked Ryan why he had not brought my car up instead of the van – I had left him my keys specifically for this purpose. He sheepishly said he would have to let the boss explain when I got back to the detachment. On the journey down I pestered the life out of him to tell me what the big secret was all about. After about half an hour he said he would tell me, but that when the boss collared me I was to act as if I knew nothing about it; I agreed.

Basically, my car had been compromised at Lynda's house and the police had received a tip-off that I was going to be shot if I was seen in the area again. The tip-off came in the form of a note sent to the RUC station that stated '*the stupid Brit bastard who drives the maroon car*', followed by the registration number of my vehicle, '*is going to get shot if he keeps parking in . . .*'. It then mentioned the exact street where Lynda lived. On arriving at the detachment I was greeted by the boss with a big grin on his face and was beckoned into his office. Who had been a naughty boy, then? The boss was quite good about the whole situation. He had met Lynda and knew I was staying there. Although he never gave me permission to do so he turned a blind eye to it. He had struck a bargain with the Special Branch inspector who had received the note to the effect that he would speak to me and try to resolve the problem.

I confirmed to the boss that I had been staying overnight at this address and that the car had been parked where the note had said. I had to hold my hands up to the situation — I had probably been quite stupid to park there consistently. However, why not turn the situation to our advantage and set up a sting? I was happy enough to act as bait, and as long as we were in control we could get a reactive result out of it. The boss looked at me and asked me if I was stark raving mad. It was known that an old boyfriend of Lynda's, whom the police knew, had apparently been making his views about me quite apparent — it was suggested by the Branch that he was behind the note. I changed the car and was a little more careful about where I parked after that. I made a promise to myself that my personal security would not slip — it was a lesson to be learnt, and I did not intend to allow myself to be faced with a similar situation ever again.

Chapter 13

Friend or Foe

The Special Branch had always been a bit of a mystery to me and the rest of the operators at our detachment. They carried out similar operations to us and were the 'sneaky-beaky' part of the police. They undertook surveillance and source-handling tasks and were eventually answerable to the same chain of command that we were. They had made it quite plain over the years that they did not need or want our assistance in any shape or form. We had tried on a few occasions to invite them up to our detachment to discuss operational deployments where we could offer them support, and on a few times had given them the opportunity to attend social nights at our bar, which were always good for a laugh. These invitations were never once taken up, and during my three years at this particular detachment I never saw a single visitor from these so-called colleagues of ours, who we were supporting in their fight against terrorism, on their patch. I was personally approached once by them, and it was an event that both shattered their mystique and confirmed to me what I already thought. They were not as clever as they liked to think they were.

I had become quite friendly with the Intelligence Officer from the local infantry regiment. His battalion had been by far the best unit I had seen operating in our area, and from an intelligence point of view they had given our detachment a lot of extremely good leads on personalities they had visited during their patrols who looked like candidates for potential source recruitments. The Intelligence Officer concerned had unusually also developed an extremely good rapport with the local Special Branch, and was well accepted by them. It was assumed by our own hierarchy that he was possibly swinging a double-edged sword for his own benefit, and was not to be trusted. So what? At least he was getting somewhere. Unknown to me, he had told two of the Special Branch officers that he considered me to be an extremely good bloke and that I was probably quite open to the offer of a joint venture if approached in the right way. They in turn secured from him an undertaking to keep this venture from their own hierarchy, and stressed that my unit was not to be aware of it either. There was something I could provide, or so they thought, which they were unable to get their own hands on. The plot thickened.

I met Roger (the IO) in his office at the base where we were both located and he asked me what I was up to that night. Did I fancy going for a few beers in town and meeting his mates from Special Branch? Apparently they had made an unusual request to meet me. I agreed, and we arranged for me to pick him up from the base later that evening. I spoke to my boss about the meeting, and he was as curious about the set-up as anyone else. He did not have a great amount of respect or trust where Roger was concerned, but was quite interested in what the outcome of the meeting would be. He spoke to our headquarters in Lisburn. Johnny, the operations officer, was away for the day, dealing with the Stevens inquiry team, which was investigating various allegations being made against certain police and military units within the Province. These units had been accused of passing classified information to terrorist organisations, allegations that were completely unfounded to my mind.

In the absence of the operations officer the boss went further up the chain-of-command and spoke to the unit's Commanding officer. He endorsed the meeting fully and agreed that it could go ahead. He would be more than interested to hear the outcome of this little clandestine get-together.

I picked Roger up at about half past eight that evening, and we headed to a small pub on the outskirts of Lisnaskea, not a particularly friendly place and certainly not the type of venue where I would normally choose to go for a few beers, especially not with policemen. Quite a few had been shot and blown up there over the years, and I was co-handler of one of our sources who lived in the place. If he were to see me then he would probably have a heart attack on the spot, especially given the company I was likely to be keeping. He would almost certainly have known the two Special Branch characters, and they definitely knew him.

I was introduced to the two covert policemen, Martin and Keith. The initial conversation mainly concerned my personal feelings about Northern Ireland. They asked how I had ended up in the job I was doing, what selection process I had gone through, and loads of other general bits and pieces. Just typical small talk. Although the chitchat seemed to be quite friendly, I got the distinct feeling that they were fishing for weak points, as policemen tend to do.

Martin in particular was quite keen to inform me that he had seen me at various places and that I was never aware that he was around or who he was. So what? The first hour was very much a game of one-upmanship, with the two of them telling me how much they knew about me and what little I knew about them.

Maybe it gave them some kind of feeling of security. It was a load of arse, really. At the end of the day I was not a threat to them either personally or otherwise, and I really could not see the point of this conversation. I was ready to get up and leave pretty soon unless there was some positive discussion to be had.

Roger eventually broke the deadlock for us about two hours later by making the remark that the two of them wanted to discuss something specific with me and that he would go to a different part of the bar to allow us to continue the conversation. Both parties agreed he could stay. They both asked me whether my unit was aware that I was meeting them, to which I replied no, this was a personal little venture, and I told them that my unit would not be very impressed with me following my own personal agenda with Special Branch. They both seemed happy with this. They asked me what I considered to be the most useful tool in the recruitment of a source, and we agreed that at the end of the day, no matter how a source was recruited, one of the main reasons they came back time and time again was the money they were paid for their information. Whatever they were paid, it was a great incentive. I did state that a number of our sources were motivated in other ways, and that money was not always the reason for them carrying out their tasks for our unit – another brownie point to the FRU! Then, after about an hour of this conversation, during which time the pints of beer started being accompanied by large Jameson chasers, the real point of the meeting came out. They had targeted a potential source for recruitment. He was ready for plucking, but they could not get their hands on any funding with which to entice him. Fine with me. What did I get from the recruitment? What amount of money did they need, and who would run the source? It appeared that the whole thing was for their benefit. They then questioned me on the availability of funds that I could lay my hands on. I could see where this was leading, and thought I would have some fun at their expense. I told them that the funds we had access to were limitless and that we kept vast amounts of ready cash in the safe at the detachment for such operations. Their eyes lit up.

They told me that they needed about £20,000, and that it would have to be kept secret from anyone else, including my own unit. How I did not fall over laughing I will never know. I said I would see what I could do and that I would get back to Roger and let them know the outcome in the next few days.

They left the pub, and shortly afterwards Roger and I headed out to the carpark. Mistrust of the Special Branch had always been a personal thing with me, and so I threw my car keys over to Roger and said he could drive. I did not relish the thought of being caught in a police vehicle checkpoint that would 'just happen' to be up the road. After all, I had about ten pints of Smithwick's in me and just about the same number of Jameson's as well. As we entered Enniskillen, there in front of us was the usual sight of the red torch waving us into a checkpoint. The policeman was known to me and Roger showed his identity card. After a general conversation we were waved on. Was this a coincidence, or was I just paranoid? I'm glad I was in the passenger seat anyway.

The following morning I spoke to the boss about the meeting and he burst out laughing when I when I told him of the request. However, if they were really going to recruit some scallywag and we could run it as a joint operation, then why not? It would have to be discussed with the head shed, though. The boss spoke to Johnny, the operations officer, who asked that I be dispatched to Lisburn to brief him on the details of my meeting. Johnny, in his usual manner, was thoroughly disgusted by the approach that had been made to me, and immediately phoned the commanding officer of Roger's regiment demanding that he be sent up to Lisburn to explain his activities. The commanding officer of our unit was away, and so the decision-making ball was in Johnny's court. He threw the idea out straight away. He considered it was deceitful and unethical for Special Branch to make such an approach, and that to use a normal army officer as an intermediate was well out of order, even for them.

On this particular occasion my back was covered. I had been through the correct channels beforehand and had kept my people informed of the situation. Johnny told me that he thought I had been led astray by a commissioned officer and that he would deal with Roger face to face. I took this personally, and told him that I was big enough to make my own decisions and did not need to be led astray by anyone, and that I still believed it to be a viable plan. With Johnny's inevitable wave of the hand I left headquarters. In all fairness I suppose he had to play everything 'by the book', and he needed the operation to be sanctioned through the correct chain of command.

The matter was never brought up again and Roger had his bollocking. I saw the two Special Branch blokes on a number of occasions in various places in the area. I nodded at them, but we never spoke. I never found out if the job went ahead or whether the source was recruited by any other means — if in fact there ever was one! The sceptical side in me was always of the opinion, and still is, that if I had been in the driving seat that night I would have had the book well and truly launched at me — I would have been out of the Province and out of the job. I am still convinced that the whole meeting was to stitch me up —

those two were just possibly devious enough to have a go at doing it. My wayward social life continued, and the rules were broken again on several occasions. But I never lost sight of rule one: Don't get caught.

Funnily enough I never did.

Chapter 14

Time to Leave

T welve years earlier I had sat in the cinema at Hohne in Germany along with a few hundred other soldiers, listening to the commanding officer's briefing about my regiment being posted to Omagh, with the same fears as any other sane person would have had on being told that they were being posted to the Province for two years. At that time the thought of going to Northern Ireland sent shivers right up my spine – I really and truly did not want to go. It was the place where soldiers got killed, by an enemy with the audacity to state they were fighting a war yet who would never show their faces as real soldiers would. These were terrorists, and terrorists can never, in my opinion, aspire to the accolade of calling themselves soldiers.

Times and attitudes change, though. Considering my initial thoughts, it was strange that as it turned out I would spend a lot longer there, especially in the role that I was lucky enough to take on, as a covert operator, after an arduous selection process embarked on entirely voluntarily! Working in an environment that demanded total professionalism was an immense learning curve – the cost of getting things wrong where human lives are at risk is one hell of a responsibility to carry. The work was fascinating, and the job satisfaction was immense.

From the information the FRU gathered from its sources innumerable lives were saved over a number of years. These people, at great risk to themselves, had been practising the so-called peace process long before Adams, McGuinness and the rest of the gang of politicians hogged the spotlight; theirs, though, is a secret peace process. Various amnesties are presently in force – convicted murderers are being released left, right and centre, their crimes forgiven by the political process, but never forgotten by the families and friends of those affected by their outrageous acts of violence. So what about the agents who provided the information to lock these people up, the agents who told us where the arms were, who was going to be killed, how the attempts would be made – will they be given an amnesty by the terrorist organisations? I really don't think so somehow. These brave people will have to keep their secret double lives clandestine for ever. They committed a crime against their own which will never be forgiven. The world of the informant is a very lonely, silent one.

The normal period of time for any British soldier to spend away from their parent regiment on a posting is usually two years. Strangely enough, for all my slagging off of Special Branch, I believe their system is the correct one – at least when they move into a job they could be there for several years. The army, however, does not follow this policy, which I generally believe to be to their detriment. I have never understood why they spend so much time and money training us for this type of work, letting us gain the experience and knowledge of the task, only to pull us out just as we are starting to be really productive. I had worked alongside some very brave people, both agents and operators. The relationship with the agents takes a lot of time and effort to build up, and for some of them the handing-over process from one operative to another can be quite traumatic. These people have relied on your guidance in how their lives should be run. It is not easy for someone to accept a new face straight away – trust has to be developed over a period of time. It is an extremely responsible task.

I had been lucky enough to have served with the unit for three years – my initial two-year tour plus a year's extension. It was early 1991, and it became obvious that my parent regiment was starting to make waves about me being returned to regimental duty. There had been an upset earlier on in the year when my extra one year's extension had been applied for. Somewhere along the line I had been 'lost' by the Royal Armoured Corps manning and records office. They had not been informed of my move to the FRU and were unaware that I had ever left the Intelligence and Security Group several years previously.

The clock was ticking away and I was due to leave the Province in June. I had been back to Germany to have a 'career' interview with the new commanding officer of my own regiment. Despite him saying that he was quite happy to have me return, and that I had the potential to make at least warrant officer, there was likely to be a catch. I had been promoted to sergeant because of my employment in Northern Ireland, but in my own regiment they still viewed me as a corporal, and it was just possible that if I returned they would have to consider returning me to that rank for a short, probationary period. The CO quite rightly informed me that while I had been away 'playing James Bond', as he put it, other people junior to me had been on their various armoured corps courses and were way ahead of me in the pecking order within my own regiment. I had not done myself any favours staying away for so long. It was time to make up my mind what I wanted.

A new RSM had taken over, with whom I got on well. A lot

of my contemporaries were now warrant officers and senior ranks, and it would have been easy to have slipped back into regimental life without the traumas of my last return some three years previously recurring. However, I had been to other places, I knew things that they did not, and I had been involved in operations that were for real and not just exercises. Every day I had faced danger from an unknown, faceless terrorist who might just have popped up when it was least expected. Yes, most of them at some time had seen service in Northern Ireland, but apart from one other bloke who had been at the FRU for a short period with me, no one had previously carried out this undercover role from my regiment for as long as I had. I knew it would be difficult for me to settle back in to life on the tank park.

I had an interview with my commanding officer in Headquarters Northern Ireland at Lisburn. He sympathised and understood my problem. He asked me if I had any ideas for the future. I told him that ideally I would like to carry on with the unit, but because of the position with my own corps and regiment I knew that this was going to be an unlikely option. The alternative was to seek similar employment, but within a civilian organisation. He asked me if I was really contemplating this avenue. I truthfully told him that if I could locate someone who would employ me with my background and training, then I would leave the army with no reservations. He told me to leave it with him and he would arrange for me to meet someone who could be of use to me, or, more to the point, to whom I might be of use.

I received a call the following Monday from the commanding officer. Could I come up to his office the following morning at ten o'clock? There was someone who wished to speak to me.

On arrival I was introduced to an immaculate gentleman who introduced himself as James. He was the head of the department in Headquarters Northern Ireland that dealt with the government's political involvement with the Province, and in particular covert operations. He was the head honcho for the security services (MI5) in the Province. He then proceeded to tell me that the CO had told him of my enquiry. He went on to list all the reasons why I should not join his organisation, how I would not fit in with or like the system they ran, how being a civil servant was a real pain in the arse, how I would probably end up with a twenty-year-old graduate as my boss (so what was new?), and how in his estimation I would not be the slightest bit happy with the whole set-up. He was obviously not their recruiting officer. I thought to myself that he was obviously trying to put me off to test my reaction and to see if I was really serious about making an approach, so I told him that for all his misgivings about his own organisation I was still very interested. He told me he would arrange another interview in due course after I had had time to reflect on what he had said.

The next time I spoke to him he again reiterated the points from the first meeting. On the whole I got the impression he was either being extremely honest with me, and really did not think I would settle into his organisation, or was just being kind and not coming straight out with the fact that he didn't want me. I would prefer to think it was the first alternative.

I had no plans other than that I had decided I would not be returning to my old regiment. Because of the routine I had been used to for the previous few years, and what I had gone through to get there, I knew it would not work out. I had decided to buy myself out of the army, but had nowhere to go. I knew I had a little time, though. I arranged my discharge date to be able to take advantage of another month's wages and to enable me to start making job applications. The boss called me into his office. He said that the signal for my discharge had been approved and I could go, no problem. My idea was basically to laze around a bit, do a bit of fishing and chase up some of the jobs that I had applied for over the period running up to my departure. The one thing I had not taken into consideration was the old catch – displacement of expectations.

When the boss said that I could go, that was exactly what he meant. I could go now – in fact, not so much *could* go, but had to go. I asked what he meant. He said that as from Friday I was out of the army; that was in precisely three days' time. Some tosser of a civil servant at the manning and records office had hit the 'delete' key on their computer and said, 'Lewis, you're off.' I was gutted! In fact the reality was quite frightening – I had never been anywhere else but in the army. I handed in my kit, my weapons, my car, and everything else I had.

The old green machine had done the hatchet job. I had lulled myself into a false sense of security by thinking that because I belonged to this large and powerful organisation and had taken risks for Queen and country I was something more than just a number. At the end of the day I was wrong. Strangely, when the dust had settled, I felt no bitterness, just disappointment that it had been so quick. In retrospect maybe it was for the best. A lot of things have happened since that Friday when I had to cadge a lift off one of my ex-fellow operators into town.

I had arrived in the Province to serve with the FRU during May 1988. During my time there I was involved in numerous covert operations. There are many operations I could not mention because of the threat to national security. Many peace deals have been tried in the past and the present peace process has at least brought Sinn Fein, representing the IRA's political stance, to the negotiating table after so long. Someone had to do it, no matter how much it sticks in the throat. However, I believe someone once said, '*When they find a solution to the Irish problem, the Irish will find another problem.*'

Omagh town, on Saturday, 15 August 1998, was to prove

that old adage correct yet again. The heinous crime committed against innocent people in the town that day, during the middle of the peace process, just proves what disgusting lengths terrorists will go to for their cause. What will happen to the murdering perpetrators of that bomb? Will they be released in a few years' time as well, in another deal for another peace process? I hope not. Enough people have died in the recent years of the Troubles. I hope there will be a total ceasefire with no more names being added to the long list of those who have already been the victims of terrorist violence.

My roots in the operational side of the FRU have been totally severed. There was no point in trying to maintain contact. The only contact I have from those days is Mike, who left shortly after me, whom I hear from frequently when he is in this country, and Ross, who gets a drunken phone call every New Year's Eve, religiously. The three amigos still keep in touch. The other members with whom I served at the detachment have all disappeared.

The unit has been brought to the attention of the media on one or two occasions, unfortunately for all the wrong reasons. I had been in Devon attending a wedding and had heard on the radio that a helicopter carrying some police and military personnel had crashed on the west coast of Scotland the previous evening. On hearing the report I made a flippant comment to my wife to the effect that the occupants had probably been going to play a golf match and were on a skive. My remark was to backfire painfully. I had returned to our hotel room with my newspaper. My wife when she saw me later, asked me if I had seen a ghost. My face was ashen. Two of the people who had died in the fateful Chinook crash that June evening were very well known to me; one was a fellow member of a services rugby team. A sad loss indeed.

A report in one of the better Sunday papers claimed that the unit had been disbanded after the Stevens Inquiry's unpublished report into the activities of one particular informant, Brian Nelson. It claimed that collusion had taken place between the FRU and Nelson, enabling him to plan murders of people thought to be members of the IRA. I had caught the tail-end of the inquiry carried out by John Stevens, then Deputy Chief Constable, but had not been involved in that particular case, nor had I any inkling of the depth of the investigation. Security within the FRU was paramount, and individual cases were never discussed with other members of the unit outside your own detachment. Knowing how the unit was run, I found the report curious to say the least. The task of the unit was to assist, by means of intelligence-gathering, the RUC in their fight against the men of violence, not to collude with or endorse such acts.

Violence and violent people had been part of my life since my early days in South Wales, from the punch-ups with the lads from other villages, and with other soldiers from different regiments while I had been in Germany, through to terrorists in Northern Ireland. Somewhere, just around the corner, there was always a chance it would happen. I had moved to England a number of months after leaving the army. The time in between had mostly been spent by the side of a river casting a fly in the hope of catching that elusive double-figured trout. He's still there somewhere. On the first evening back on the mainland I was up to my neck in boxes and packing materials with no time to fit in making a meal. I headed into the local shopping area and parked up just down the road from a Kentucky Fried Chicken takeaway. After I had collected my order I headed back to my car. Suddenly there was a commotion and lots of shouting going on behind me. I turned to watch as two men wearing Balaclavas and carrying sawn-off shotguns ran into the take-away. I watched intently as I sat in my vehicle in the dark. After all the years of waiting for something like this to happen when I was in a position to deal with it, I had to sit it out. I noted the registration of the car as it sped up the road and went straight through the red lights on the crossing. I went to a telephone box and made an anonymous call to the police, told them the number and then drove home to eat my takeaway.

It was not to be the only brush with violence I was to have within a short period of leaving the Province. Some time later I was heading out of London to drive down to Wales for a meeting I was attending the following day. I thought I would use the quiet time late that evening for easy driving, and made my way along the North Circular towards the start of the M1. I spotted a blue-flashing light in my rear-view mirror. A police motorbike went hurtling past me on the clear road, then a police van and car followed in hot pursuit of their bike-riding colleague. I joked to myself that they had probably just finished their shifts and were off home for supper. As I approached the area of Staples Corner I was flagged down. I was the only car on the road. The police motorcyclist informed me that the road up ahead was blocked and that I would have to find an alternative route through the back roads to continue my journey. Then there was a muffled boom from a few hundred metres further up the road. 'Well, it's well blocked now,' I said to the policeman. He went into a major flap, shouting at me to reverse and get out of the area quickly. It all seemed strangely familiar. I continued on my way.

A lot had happened in the Province during my service with my regiment, the Group and the FRU. In the course of various stints in Northern Ireland there were over 4,000 shooting incidents, over 2,500 explosions, 380 civilian deaths and a total of 218 RUC, UDR and British Army personnel killed. A damning and thought-provoking set of figures.

With my fingers crossed, I cannot help thinking back to my schooldays and our gang's little motto. Rule one: don't get caught.

Glossary

AK47   Assault rifle originally of Soviet design favoured by terrorist units.

ASU   Active Service Unit. A unit within the IRA which carries out terrorist operations.

BOX   Nickname of MI5, the security service responsible for high-level security matters within Great Britain and Northern Ireland.

CO   Commanding Officer. Usually a lieutenant-colonel in rank.

COT   Close Observation Troop (or platoon). A sub-unit of a regiment trained for long-term observations.

CQB   Close-Quarter Battle. Term given to weapons training and used in conjunction with self-defence techniques.

DET   Detachment. Nickname given to both 14 Int and FRU locations.

DS   Directing Staff. A body of instructors.

DSM   Detachment Sergeant-Major. A warrant officer at each detachment responsible for the day-to-day running of all aspects of operations and administration.

E2	An operator who is from an all-arms background, i.e. not Intelligence Corps.
FRU	Force Research Unit. A specialist unit within the British Army which carries out source-handling operations.
HK	Heckler and Koch. A German-designed weapon used by specialist units.
HQNI	Headquarters Northern Ireland.
IO	Intelligence Officer. Term used by both the British Army and terrorist organisations for the person responsible for routine intelligence tasking.
IRA	Irish Republican Army. The main terrorist organisation within Northern Ireland.
NAAFI	Navy, Army & Air Force Institute. The soldier's café, bar and leisure place.
NCO	Non-Commissioned Officer. A soldier of rank from lance-corporal to warrant officer.
NI	Northern Ireland.
PT	Physical Training.
QRF	Quick Reaction Force. A stand-by unit from any regiment which is ready for immediate deployment.
RHQ	Regimental Headquarters.
RSM	Regimental Sergeant-Major.
RUC	Royal Ulster Constabulary. The police force in Northern Ireland.
SAFN	Belgian made Fabrique Nationale 'Saive' rifle.
SAS	Special Air Service. A special forces unit within the British Army.
SB	Special Branch. A specialist unit within the police which carries out surveillance and source-handling amongst other tasks.
SDLP	Social Democratic and Labour Party. Nationalist constitutional party.

Sinn Fein	The political party that represents the IRA. Originally meaning 'We Ourselves'.
SIW	Specialist Intelligence Wing. The training establishment for FRU operators.
SLR	Self-Loading Rifle.
SMLE	Short Magazine Lee-Enfield rifle.
TCG	Tasking Co-ordination Group. A unit consisting of both police and army personnel who co-ordinate operations throughout the Province.
UDR	Ulster Defence Regiment. Former name of the Royal Irish Regiment, the youngest and largest regiment in the British Army.
VCP	Vehicle Check Point.
14 Int.	A specialist unit within the British Army which carries out passive covert surveillance operations.